FAIRACRES P

Towards a Theology of Psychotherapy

The Spirituality of Wendy Robinson

Andrew Louth

SLG Press

© 2024 SLG Press
First Edition 2024

Fairacres Publications No. 212

Print ISBN 978-0-7283-0372-0
Fairacres Publications Series ISSN 0307-1405

Edited and typeset in Palatino Linotype by Julia Craig-McFeely

Biblical quotations are taken from the New Revised Standard Version of
the Bible unless otherwise noted

SLG Press
Convent of the Incarnation
Fairacres • Oxford
www.slgpress.co.uk

Printed by
Grosvenor Group Ltd, Loughton, Essex

CONTENTS

---◆---

---◆---

PREFACE

This volume along with its companion volume, *Cosmos, Crisis &
Christ: Essays of Wendy Robinson*,[1] pay tribute to the life and work of
Wendy Robinson. A companion, what better word to describe Wendy,
for whom being there for the other, through thick and thin, was at
the core of her life and faith. The expanse and variety of Wendy's life
and work and, thereby, contacts, is itself testimony to her self-forget-
ting presence. It would be true to say that Wendy's life was oral rather
than written, which is quite an irony given the significance of literature and poetry in her life. Wendy responded in depth to the person
in front of her giving her full attention to that which was said and
that which was left unspoken. The essays gathered in this volume reflect this oral tradition, some of which have been transcribed from
talks she gave. Is there a coherence to the collection? Yes. We would
not be doing justice to Wendy's actual sense of her vocation and life
if her exploration of 'the self', to use short-hand for her psychotherapeutic work, was not held in the light of her faith journey. They were
bound up with one another.

On being asked about her prayer life she replied that when she
was seated with someone during a therapy session, she tried to open
her heart to the fullness of the person before her, just as she did when
standing before God in prayer. In this opening of her heart she let the
other enter in, received them and listened deeply to the hidden voice.
In this labour she said she was never alone, but open to the numinous
presence of the Other/other, whom she could neither have or hold,
but could receive in relationship. Her work was her prayer. Prayer

---

[1] Collected and edited by Andrew Louth, Fairacres Publications 211
(Oxford: SLGPress, 2024).

was her work. And this prayer took her into dark and socially 'off bounds' contexts. Working on the back wards of large psychiatric hospitals taught her to listen into the seeming madness for the truth and insight revealed therein. Reflecting on why some people 'break down' she commented that for some it is the sheer fact of being asked to carry a psychic reality that is too big for them, and which in truth can only be borne by God. This was their suffering: to be participant in a reality that was far greater than most of us ever know., and maybe on our behalf.

Narrative is the linking thread throughout these essays, the narrative of our lives within the narrative of the life of the Word made flesh, Jesus Christ. May the gloriously embodied and down to earth wisdom of Wendy shine through these words, as the light of Christ shone in all her encounters.

Mother Katharine Hall ssc
Ty-Mawr Convent, Gwent

NOTES

A number of works by Wendy Robinson are reproduced in a new edition as a companion volume to this book: *Cosmos, Crisis & Christ: Essays of Wendy Robinson*, collected and edited by Andrew Louth, Fairacres Publications 211 (SLG Press 2024). Citations to the following works therefore refer to this new edition.

Exploring Silence, Fairacres Publications 170 (Oxford: SLG Press, 2013), new edition in *Cosmos, Crisis & Christ*, 63–92.

A Journey to the Russian Orthodox Church: An Ecumenical Journey into Orthodoxy (London: Servants of Christ the King Pamphlets, 2007), new edition in *Cosmos, Crisis & Christ*, 1–16.

The Lost Traveller's Dream: Developing a Theology for Working with Mental Illness, Occasional Papers in Christian Counselling, no. 1 (Oxford: Oxford Christian Institute for Counselling, 1995), new edition in *Cosmos, Crisis & Christ*, 33–48.

'Mary, the Flower and Fruit of Worship: The Mother of God in the Orthodox Tradition', in *Abba: The Tradition of Orthodoxy in the West. Festschrift for Bishop Kallistos Ware*, ed. John Behr, Andrew Louth, Dimitri Conomos (Crestwood, NY: SVSP, 2003), 193–205, new edition in *Cosmos, Crisis & Christ*, 93–108.

'The Quest for the Heart of the Work: An Ontological Approach to Spirituality and Psychotherapy/Counselling', *Psychodynamic Counselling* 4/3 (August 1998), 335–48, new edition in *Cosmos, Crisis & Christ*, 17–32.

Sounding Stones: Reflections on the Mystery of the Feminine, Fairacres Publications 99 (Oxford: SLG Press, 1987), new edition in *Cosmos, Crisis & Christ*, 49–62.

TOWARDS A THEOLOGY OF PSYCHOTHERAPY

THE SPIRITUALITY OF WENDY ROBINSON

INTRODUCTION

I have to confess that I am not at all sure what I am doing in this essay. It is based—so far as literary resources are concerned—almost entirely on pamphlets written by Wendy Robinson, mostly published by the Guild of Pastoral Psychology, the Society of Christ the King, of which she was Warden from 2009–13, or by the Sisters of the Love of God, the Anglican contemplative community with which she had a long association, its Mother House being in East Oxford—either in the *Fairacres Chronicle* or as a *Fairacres Pamphlet*.[1] My memories of Wendy also inform what I am writing, but I suspect in an unsystematic, and even undetectable, way. I knew Wendy from some time in the early 1970s until her death, though not very well to begin with. I don't think an account of my friendship with Wendy over the years would be appropriate here, save to say that when I became Orthodox in 1989, Wendy was my godmother; as that, and in other ways, I owe her a lot. What I have done in the following pages is to build up some picture of her approach to things, of her thought, you might say. This has not been easy, as I think our ways of thinking were very different, even though at many points our interests overlapped. Furthermore, it is clear from the written material on which I have based my account

---

[1] These resources are invaluable, but have limitations. Some seem to have been seen through the press by Wendy—the Fairacres pamphlets and the publications by the Guild of Pastoral Psychology, for example—others seem to be transcriptions from recordings of talks given by Wendy without any evidence of her correcting them. One, *Windows for the Soul: Living with Icons* (London: Servants of Christ the King, 2007, Printed 2020), has notes by the long-suffering transcriber, WS (who?), who at one point, cued to the word *disponible*, notes: 'My subeditors cant [*sic*] find this in the dictionary but I think she might be talking French!' (*Windows for the Soul*, 15, n. 4).

that Wendy—as I was already well aware—communicated best in speaking (though it might be truer to say, through her *listening*, for with groups that she had been invited to address, one often felt a profound sense of her silence—a silence that elicited from other people thoughts and feelings in a way that often surprised them, sometimes barely known to them, and a silence from which her own words quite evidently originated). Her writing—like her handwriting in letters and suchlike—was impulsive and impressionistic, though capable of rare passages of analytic preciseness, held together not by any normal syntax, but by dashes. The word 'parataxis' might have been coined to capture something of the nature of her prose style. Although by no means without rational argument and structure, her thought proceeded more by way of imagination—symbols, metaphors, and leaps of … imagination—for though there was nothing in the way of poetry in the material Mother Katharine Hall (Reverend Mother of Ty Mawr Convent in Wales) sent me shortly after Wendy's death, she was a capable poet, and was very pleased when one of her poems was published in the journal, *Agenda*.[2] What follows is, for all these reasons and others, very much an essay: tentative, an attempt to draw together themes scattered throughout her writings into some sort of coherent and patterned structure. I only hope that those who knew Wendy better than I, will recognize her from these reflections.

---

[2] 'Autolycus: Old Crow', *Agenda*, vol. 43, nos. 2–3 (Spring 2008), 96–7. The poem is reproduced below, pp. 62–3.

1
BRIEF BIOGRAPHY

Wendy Pannell Robinson (née Flintoff) was born in Barnsley on 1 July 1934 and died on 12 December 2013 in Exeter, aged 79. Her father, Arthur Godfrey Flintoff (*b.* 1907), a solicitor and the Deputy Town Clerk of Barnsley County Borough Council, tragically died on 2 May 1936, leaving his wife May, née Fairgrieve (22 May 1909–20 May 2005), and two-year old daughter, Wendy. A little later, May married Thomas ('Tod') Patterson, a tenant farmer in Newsham and it was in this small village at Hill Top Farm, in the Yorkshire Dales on the edge of the Pennines, that Wendy spent her childhood. On 24 February 1939 Wendy was presented with a sister Jillianne: the warmth and humour of Jill was a source of great joy and comfort to Wendy —particularly in the years after Wendy left Yorkshire:

I was brought up on a sheep farm in the Yorkshire Dales with a lot of mystical experience of transcendence and a sense of presence on those grand moors. There was a reciprocal invocation between the Spirit and the 'Spirit-in-the-wind' which always blew. My identification with Emily Brontë went deep. Fortunately I never found Heathcliff! Then I went West to university in Bristol with all that softening of scenery and climate that was quite difficult to tangle with at first; me with my Pennine backbone and my three adjectives—Good; Bad; Nobbut middlin. The speech seemed so flowery.[3]

Wendy was thus brought up on a remote farm, which also gave her time to read. Her Flintoff grandfather owned a bookshop in Sunderland and kept her well stocked with books. Wendy was a prodigious reader of the classics by candlelight and torch, and in later life identified the 'bookshop gene' in her sons and grandchildren. Wendy was educated at schools in nearby Richmond, participating in school activities, notably playing Dido in Purcell's opera in 1949, as well as joining the Girl Guides, and representing the North of England at a conference in Paris about social welfare and civic values. For her Advanced Level General Certificate of Education (GCE A-levels) Wendy studied Latin, French and English Literature.

It is difficult to appreciate today, what the impact of winning a place at Bristol University to read English Literature must have had on the then eighteen-year-old 'Yorkshire lass' that Wendy was in 1952. Wendy clearly saw this as an escape. Her deep love for Yorkshire—the sight of the heather and the soul song of the curlew—were ever-present throughout her life. Something that could always be returned to, but which could never again tie her, a place that would in many ways always be 'home' but not somewhere she could ever live. Her frequent visits to Yorkshire were a great joy, and a source of rejuvenation and energy—before returning to the life she had created elsewhere.

---

[3] Wendy Robinson, 'A Journey to the Russian Orthodox Church: An Ecumenical Journey into Orthodoxy', in *Cosmos, Crisis & Christ: Essays of Wendy Robinson*, collected and edited by Andrew Louth, Fairacres Publications 211 (Oxford: SLG Press, 2024), 2–3.

At the age of twenty-one, Wendy acquired her first car—and bought a tractor for her stepfather—as the result of a small inheritance from her father's family in Sunderland, and this car marked the end of her time in the isolated North Yorkshire Dales. Her car, then and later, became for her a symbol of freedom.

At Bristol University she studied under L. C. Knights, delighted in poetry, and wrote a paper on Gerard Manley Hopkins's 'The Wreck of the Deutschland'. Her tutors often remarked that whilst the work was good and interesting the handwriting was difficult to read, and the sentences and thoughts strung out with dashes! That never changed. During her time at university, Wendy became involved in socialism, Jungian psychology, and, after a conversion experience, embraced Evangelical Anglicanism (a development from the Methodism of her upbringing). After her graduation in 1955, she stayed on for a further year to gain a Post-Graduate Certificate in Education.

In this year, through her friendship with Professor R. C. Wilson, she came to know the Quakers, with their combination of social concern and experience of silent worship. It must have been around this time that Wendy became a member of the Society of Friends: she is recorded as a member of the Bristol Park Street Meeting in 1960 (giving, as her address in London: 105 Elgin Crescent, W 11); it seems likely she joined the Quakers in 1958/9, but seems to have left by 1962.[4] Her first teaching post was at an Approved School for teenage girls in Calne, Wiltshire. In 1959, Wendy returned to Bristol to study for a Diploma in Social Science and then went on to the London School of Economics to complete the Certificate in Psychiatric Social Work, studying under D. W. Winnicott and attending lectures by R. D. Laing. Then followed a period at St Bernard's Hospital, Southall, where she had special responsibilities in the Alcoholic Unit and the Neurosis Unit. There she encountered Jewish psychiatrists and her interest in Jewish thought was kindled, especially the thinking of Martin Buber.

---

[4] Information from Gregory Bridge: e-mail, 1 July 2014.

In 1963, Wendy took up a post as Lecturer in English and Social Studies, Serowe Teacher Training College, Bechuanaland (now Botswana), Africa. On the boat out, she met Edward Robinson, whom she later married. He was a scion of an Anglican clerical family, his elder brother being John Robinson, then Bishop of Woolwich. Despite serious illness, Wendy stayed on in Africa, and spent a Christmas break with Edward at Salisbury in Southern Rhodesia (now Harare in Zimbabwe), where she met the Dean of the Anglican Cathedral there, Gonville ffrench-Beytagh, who became a great friend. Through him, Wendy found herself drawn to the sacramental life of High Anglicanism, as well as to the practice of contemplative prayer; it was ffrench-Beytagh who introduced her to the Jesus Prayer.

In 1964, Wendy moved from Bechuanaland to Northern Rhodesia, now Zambia, and took up a post as Social Worker for the government of Northern Rhodesia with special responsibility for Alcoholics on the Copperbelt. Later that year, Edward and Wendy were married. Two of their sons were born in Africa, which they left in 1967 to return to England. After two years in Cheltenham, where their youngest son was born, they settled in Oxford in 1970. Wendy was involved in various voluntary activities during the first ten years of her marriage; she then resumed her career as a psychotherapist, establishing a practice in 1975. She also continued lecturing. In Oxford she came to know the Sisters of the Love of God, with their Mother House at Fairacres in East Oxford. She also began to encounter Orthodoxy. This came about partly through participating in events at the Orthodox centre in Canterbury Road, Oxford, but more deeply through the deep friend-ships she formed—with Nicolas and Militza Zernov, and the then Archimandrite Kallistos Ware. When travelling to London to teach she had a further opportunity to visit and receive counsel from Fr Lev Gillet. She also formed a close relationship with Mother Maria, Mother Thekla, and Mother Katherine, visiting them in their monastery first in Filgrave, Buckinghamshire, and latterly in Normanby, Yorkshire.

In 1980, she became Orthodox, received into the Russian juris-diction by Fr Kallistos Ware, himself a priest of the Greek jurisdiction.

Her godmother was Militza Zernov. Later Wendy spoke of what she found in Orthodoxy, and the way that it connected with her practice of psychotherapy:

> The length and depth of its worship, its rich symbolism, its teaching of the way of silence and stillness in prayer gets underneath all that I do in my work as a psychotherapist—with symptoms, nightmares and deep personal journeyings.[5]

She also spoke of the importance of antinomies, which she learnt from Militza: the realization 'that the faith could only be expressed through profound opposites which have to be held in tension—creative, life-giving, sometimes crucifying in their intensity'.[6] Deepening this intuition concerning antinomies, she quoted Fr Lev Gillet (who actually died on the day she was received into Orthodoxy), who had said:

> O strange Orthodox church, so poor and so weak … maintained as if by miracle through so many vicissitudes and struggles; Church of contrasts, so traditional and yet at the same time so free, so archaic and yet so alive, so ritualistic and yet so personally mystical; Church where the Evangelical pearl of great price is preciously guarded— yet often beneath a layer of dust. Church which has so frequently proved incapable of action, yet which knows as does no other, how to sing the joy of Pascha.[7]

As a member of the Russian Orthodox Church in England, she played an active role, not just in local worship, but also at a national level, being a member of the Council of the Diocese of Sourozh (and later of the Vicariate) and involved in the recommendation of candidates for priesthood. She often spoke at the annual diocesan conferences

---

[5] 'Journey', 5.

[6] Idem, 7.

[7] Ibid. From a sermon delivered at an anniversary service for his friend, Archimandrite Irénée Winnaert, in February 1938: this passage quoted in Elisabeth Behr-Sigel, *Un Moine de l'Église d'Orient: le père Lev Gillet* (Paris: Cerf, 1993), 173.

and was a participating member of the Fellowship of St John the Baptist and the Association of Orthodox Christian Psychotherapists, as well as of the Fellowship of St Alban and St Sergius. For ten years, 1983–1993, Wendy was Lecturer in Pastoral Psychology at Ripon College, Cuddesdon. This was a task that she really enjoyed and she kept in contact with many of the students as they moved into ministry.

Wendy was involved in many other activities, but she came to have a special role in relation to religious communities, both Anglican and Roman Catholic, as a psychotherapist, and also spiritual counsellor, giving talks and retreats. She had a deep belief that the lives of these men and women were essential to the well-being of all. She was therefore aware of the importance of enabling the members of these communities to deepen their self-understanding and be aware of the gifts and shadows of living together in enclosed/apostolic single-sex communities.[8]

In 1991 Wendy and Edward left Oxford and moved to Hope Mansell on the edge of the Forest of Dean; this move was occasioned by Edward's desire for more space within which to pursue his creative work as a sculptor (having retired from research) and gardening.[9] There Wendy established her first 'Wendy-Hut' in the garden (the second was in Exeter), where she met friends and clients. After fourteen years, in 2005, they moved to Exeter, where it was easier for Edward who had to cope with increasing blindness. Wendy was also closer to her grandchildren; the role of grandmother was one she took seriously and with great delight. After forty-nine years of marriage, Wendy's husband, Edward, died at home in Exeter on 30 May 2013. Wendy did not long survive him, dying on 12 December in the same year.[10]

---

[8] See, especially, 'Sounding Stones: Reflections on the Mystery of the Feminine', *Cosmos, Crisis & Christ*, 49–62.

[9] Edward moved in a different direction theologically, from High Church Anglicanism to nonconformity and finally the Quakers.

[10] This first, biographical part reproduces, with some additions, the obituary I wrote for *Sobornost* 36/1 (2014), 92–6.

2
'AN HONEST WOMAN'

Several times Wendy said (and from the way she said it, it sounds like a trope to which she had frequent recourse) that her embrace of Orthodox Christianity and her practice as a psychotherapist had made an 'honest woman' of her. I sense that she meant this at several levels, but the basic one was that her coming to accept two ways of life—Orthodox Christianity and psychotherapy—could be united in her personal being, and this made an 'honest woman' of her, one who did not need to pretend that these aspects of her life were separate. For in both cases, there are strong voices that want to keep them apart: the view of some believers that profession of any faith, let alone something so all-embracing as the Orthodox Christian faith, rules out any recourse to psychotherapy as illegitimate, even a betrayal of one's faith, while it is a principle of much psychotherapeutic practice that any explicit acknowledgment of faith, of any kind, is inappropriate and needs, at least, to be 'bracketed off'.

One place where this trope occurs is in a passage about her experience of the Orthodox liturgy in her autobiographical reflections, 'A Journey to the Russian Orthodox Church—an ecumenical journey to Orthodoxy.'[1] There she says that

> The liturgy got right underneath all that I was working with as a psychotherapist—people's pathologies of soul, of psyche, addictive compulsive habits, existential anxieties and my own symptoms and nightmares and failures in love. I could let them all go into the Liturgy and find myself sustained from a very deep level. It was nourishing and challenging. I sometimes say that it made an honest woman out of me—not to live in the two language and experience

---

[1] In *Cosmos, Crisis & Christ*, 1–16.

worlds of depth psychology and faith, but being called, led, driven to bring them together ... But as one learns to let go and let be and let God ... one finds deep internal rhythms of the liturgical life almost as deepening as inner silence. One begins to understand that it all sustains me rather than me having to sustain it. It understands me and I do not always have to understand it. And anyway what is called this CATAPHATIC way, the way of affirmation and use of images, is all the time opened into the APOPHATIC way—the way of living from the mysteries of divine Love, Truth and Mercy that are beyond all concepts and words.[2]

What made Wendy an 'honest woman' was not, note, some *argument* about the compatibility of depth psychology and faith, but an *experience* of the 'deep internal rhythms' of the Liturgy, and the life flowing from the Liturgy, something made even clearer by her interpretation of this in terms of the contrast and complementarity of what are called 'cataphatic' and 'apophatic' theology—affirmative and negative theology: a distinction that emphasizes the way in which these two apparently opposing ways of approaching God flow one into the other, and are to be understood at a level far different from the logical dichotomy in terms of which apophatic/cataphatic theology is often presented.

Elsewhere Wendy speaks of having been made an 'honest woman'. An example can be found in a more directly psychological pamphlet: 'The Quest for the Heart of the Work: An Ontological Approach to Spirituality and Psychotherapy/Counselling', an article published in *Psychodynamic Counselling*.[3] At one point Wendy remarks:

---

[2] This section of 'Journey' is called: 'Let go, Let be, Let God'. 'Journey', 9.

[3] 'The Quest for the Heart of the Work: An Ontological Approach to Spirituality and Psychotherapy/Counselling', in *Cosmos, Crisis & Christ*, 17–34. It is relatively exceptional to find in the Wendy dossier conventionally published, rather than privately printed, articles. With the published articles, as in this case, one can be sure of the date given; the privately printed articles seem often to have been printed on demand, so that the dates perhaps refer to the moment of printing.

I used to say to the students that ontology was making an honest woman out of me—bringing about a complex, challenging and often conflictual marriage between the worlds that I had all too often kept separate for the sake of a somewhat dishonest peace.[4]

What is striking here is what it is that Wendy says has made an honest woman of her: ontology. It sounds a very cerebral word for Wendy to use, but use it she does, repeatedly. A few lines before the quotation she explains the provenance of the word, introducing it as a key term that enabled the Westminster Pastoral Foundation to find sufficient common ground to become a coherent enterprise:

We searched long and hard for a word that could hold for us the necessary sustained attention to the mystery of being and human being. We believed that this mystery always surpasses and eludes our attempts both to know all about things, and the theories and methodologies in psychodynamic work that guide us as to how to do something with what is presented to us. Eventually we settled, with a sense of gravity and perhaps foolhardiness, on a word with a long philosophical history—ontology: the science and study of being.[5]

The realms bridged by this focus on ontology were the realm of Jungian (or at least Jungian-inspired) psychotherapy and Christian spiritual counselling: the Jungian dimension is alluded to by Wendy herself when she introduces her collaborator in this endeavour, David Holt, as a Jungian analytical psychologist (she describes herself in the contributor's details as a 'Jungian psychotherapist'). A sense that Jung, rather than Freud, would provide a more sympathetic partner for Christian pastoral and spiritual counselling—or Christian engagement with modern psychology, generally—was widespread in Christian circles in the latter half of the twentieth century: such a conviction formed the basis of the Guild of Pastoral Psychology; I am not sure that it was very securely based. In so far as the notion of ontology is concerned, this is something we shall

[4] 'Quest', 21.
[5] Idem, 20.

11

consider further, when we explore the way Wendy's thoughts on this were developed alongside David Holt.

What I shall seek to do now is pursue the two partners in Wendy's 'complex, challenging and often conflictual marriage' between psychotherapy and faith, exploring each side for its own sake for, as in a marriage, the two partners had their own lives and traditions which they shared without surrendering one to another, or without there being any blending that erased their individuality.

3
ORTHODOXY

I have called this section 'Orthodoxy', as this is where Wendy's spiritual journey led; this journey did not, of course, end in Orthodoxy, but rather continued in a new, and certainly for Wendy richer, environment: as she remarks, 'I became Orthodox in 1980. It has been right for me.'[1] (She goes on to list the reasons she gave in the first passage cited about her being made 'an honest woman'.) She begins her account of her journey to the Russian Orthodox Church by saying, 'I am a walking ecumenical movement', for she had passed through several forms of Christianity on her way to Orthodoxy. She had been born a Methodist, when it was still the religion of the dales and moors, the pit villages and the industrial towns and cities of the North East of England. Later, at university, she became an Evangelical convert, experiencing the living Christ and committing her life to him, learning to 'read the Bible and to pray and go on believing that Christ is "able to keep that which I have committed unto Him" (2 Tim. 1:12)'.[2] There followed a brief, but compelling, period with the Quakers, where she learnt not only the meaning of silence (that 'fitted in the moors'), but also a way of believing that included profound social thinking, leading her to become an anti-nuclear marcher and demonstrator for political freedoms. It was with the Quakers, too, that she found support in her confrontation with corruption in authority figures encountered in her own work as teacher of difficult children and in hospital, through which she learnt to 'speak truth to power'.[3] She embraced High

---

[1] 'Journey', 5.
[2] Cf. 'Journey', 3.
[3] Ibid.

Church Anglicanism when she was in Southern Africa, where she met her husband, Edward, as well as the charismatic High-Anglican priest, Gonville ffrench-Beytagh, who had a profound influence on her, drawing her into 'a sacramental church. I went on learning about Life, Prayer, God, from that dear and beloved man, who was without doubt the finest pastoral priest I have ever met'.[4]

Finally, after a decade in Oxford, Orthodoxy. Wendy did not, however, pass *through* all these different ways of being Christian, leaving them behind, as it were; they all remained with her: the Methodism of her youth, in the wildness of the Pennine Dales; the commitment she learnt from the Evangelicals; the depth and truth, nourished in silence, expressed in social witness of the Quakers; and then the high sacramental Anglicanism in the Church in Southern Africa, with its strong and costly witness against racial injustice. All this remained with her, as part of her being, as a member of the Orthodox Church. A 'walking ecumenical movement', indeed, or maybe better: a 'living ecumenical movement'.

What did Orthodoxy mean to her? The 'Journey' is intended to clarify this, and what emerges is, in some respects, all too unsurprising.

- Antinomy: the sense, learnt from her godmother, Militza Zernov, that 'the faith could only be expressed through profound opposites which have to be held in tension—creative, life-giving, sometimes crucifying in their intensity'.[5] This was affirmed, too, by Fr Lev Gillet, originally a French Catholic whose route to Orthodoxy led him to become a monk at the Benedictine monastery of Farnborough, through ministry as a Greek Catholic priest in Poland, where he was ordained priest by Metropolitan Sheptytsky, then back to Paris, where he was received into the Russian Orthodox Church through concelebration: Wendy quotes his acclamation of a Church as a texture of antinomies, which is given above in the brief biographical section.

---

[4] 'Journey', 4.
[5] Idem, 6–7.

- The spiritual life, with its emphasis on repentance and commitment to the guiding of the Holy Spirit, humility, and what the Russians call *umilenie*, 'tender loving compassion in all humility and acknowledgment of what makes us truly lovingly human together'.[6] The peculiar architectural form of traditional Orthodox church-buildings — 'not Gothic but domed, perhaps nearer to the early Romanesque than our style in the West [which] helps the spirit too; rounded, earthed, like the Spirit hovering and brooding over the deeps of the cosmos and of human beings; the abyss of our being called out to the abyss of God's love'.[7]

- Beauty — from Dostoevsky: 'Beauty will save the world';[8] 'Beauty is attractive. It has drawing power — the power of God's love...'[9] — but 'The shadow side is that the beauty can attract just on the aesthetic level and that becomes thin unless the beauty draws us to the strong mercy of God's love and to how our participation in divine things leads to our deification. 'Deification' is a strong and demanding word in Orthodoxy that resonates with the Western word, sanctification.'[10]

- Apophatic/cataphatic theology: This we have already encountered, and noted that for Wendy it is less a contrast between thinking of God in terms of negation (apophatic) or affirmation (cataphatic), but in terms of experience in which two ways — affirmation of God's revelation and an accompanying sense of a need to transcend our understanding by denying it — are encountered as contrasting ways of approaching God that flow one into the other. In this sense, the apophatic/kataphatic distinction is closely akin to the idea of antinomy.

- The *epiklesis* (invocation) of the Holy Spirit in the Divine Liturgy; the importance of invocation of the Spirit to remedy the dulling

---

[6] 'Journey', 8.

[7] Idem, 8.

[8] An assertion attributed to Prince Myshkin in Dostoevsky, *The Idiot*, Part 3, ch. 5, trans. Richard Pevear and Larissa Volokhonsky (London: Everyman's Library, 2002), 382; quoted by Wendy frequently, e.g. 'Journey', 8, 12.

[9] An expansion of the saying from Dostoevsky: see 'Journey', 12.

[10] 'Journey', 8.

effect of custom, which can form what 'Paul Evdokimov calls a "suit of armour" guarding us from the living spirit and Fr Lev called a "layer of dust"'.[11]

- *Sobornost*—an untranslatable term derived from the Slavonic translation of 'catholic' in the Creed—conveying a sense of the mutual coinherence of all Christians with one another through participation in Christ in the one Church.

- 'The central dogmas—belief in the holy Trinity and the Incarnation of the God Man—underpin the spirituality of the Church'.[12]

- The communion of saints—Mary the Mother of God: no dogmas about her, rather 'the flower and fruit of worship ripened in tradition':[13] something Wendy developed in her essay, 'Mary: the Fruit and Flower of Worship. The Mother of God in the Orthodox Tradition'.[14]

- The sense of the cosmos, expressed liturgically in so many ways: at the Transfiguration and especially in the blessing of the Waters at Theophany, with its invocation of 'Sun, Moon, Stars, Heights and Depths, all the Cosmos and the "dragons of the deep"', 'the life-giving Cross plunged into the waters, three times, to represent new life not just for us but for the whole cosmos in Christ'—'an experience of NEXUS MYSTERIORUM—the way all truths interact and cohere'.[15]

- The Jesus Prayer—which Wendy knew in a slightly unusual form: 'Lord Jesus Christ, Son of *the living* God, have mercy on me a sinner'—not a mantra, but an invocation, a prayer to the Lord Jesus Christ, which the Spirit can pray in us. 'At first', Wendy says, 'I was not sure of it and certainly for many it is interspersed with other forms of personal prayer'.[16]

---

[11] Idem, 10.

[12] 'Journey', 12.

[13] Idem, 13; cf. Wendy Robinson, *Windows for the Soul. Living with Icons* (London: Servants of Christ the King, 2007), 17–18.

[14] In *Cosmos, Crisis & Christ*, 93–108.

[15] 'Journey', 13.

[16] Idem, 14.

I began by saying that what Orthodoxy meant to Wendy might seem 'unsurprising'—nevertheless, it is all shot through by a kind of attention to, or expectation of, a deeper sense, where everything meets and all is illuminated and illuminating.

4
ORTHODOXY: ICONS

There is another talk by Wendy, introducing her audience to Orthodoxy, but this time in a more focused way—through icons, 'windows for the soul'. The first pages are as much an introduction to Orthodoxy as to icons, for Westerners who might, she suggests, feel a mixture of 'understanding, empathy—and baffled attraction'. She speaks of the way figures in an icon seem rather distant, hieratic, 'not immediately accessible to feeling ..., [but] standing ... as some kind of central image representing objective truths of the faith'. Nevertheless, icons play an 'intimate part in [Orthodox] people's lives from birth to death', given as presents at baptism, and placed in the open coffin. They are also found in Orthodox homes in a special icon corner (or 'beautiful corner'), where lamps and candles are burnt, and incense offered, before the icons. Wendy explains the peculiar way (peculiar, that is, to Westerners, though in fact the most ancient practice) in which Orthodox Christians make the sign of the cross, with the horizontal stroke passing from the right shoulder to the left, in contrast to the Western stroke passing from the left to the right. She explains the distinction between veneration, which can be offered to anything worthy, and worship, only offered to God. Finally, icons can be thought of as WINDOWS into an invisible world; MAGNETS, drawing us, making us make the turn, the TESHUVAH (Hebrew equivalent of the Greek μετάνοια), the 'repentant move towards God'; or a BURNING GLASS, 'helping us to feel the fire, the warmth of God's love'.[1]

---

[1] Summary of *Windows*, 1–6.

That is Wendy's introduction to icons, but I have missed something out. The talk on icons was illustrated by icons Wendy had brought with her; these icons illustrate, or even embody the presentation of Orthodoxy in the talk. But the first illustration came at the very beginning, even before the introduction I have just summarized; not an icon as such, it was a large colour photograph of a 7-month old foetus in the mother's womb—'the foetal sack like a halo and the entire effect stark, the infant very much alive, its tiny hands held up as if in blessing'—a picture, Wendy suggested, of 'the mystery of something made in the image of God, so wonderfully portrayed in that veiled figure yet to appear in the outside world'. Wendy remarked that 'so many people, particularly women, have talked with me about feeling that somewhere in the spiritual world they are pregnant with the unspoken—something that has yet to come to birth and to speak, to find a way'. Perhaps this picture of a foetus helps us to understand something deeper about the icon, some feminine dimension, hitherto unsuspected. However, Wendy brought this preface to the introduction to a close, saying, 'but anyway let us keep in mind then that sense of the human being made in the depths of the womb, in the image of God'.[2]

The first icon she discusses is of the Nativity of Christ,[3] and she drew the attention of her group first of all to the Mother of God, seeming 'to face away from the child, and out into the world', perhaps 'seeing, even from the beginning, the future, the cross'. And then Joseph, represented in a corner of the icon, almost outside the scene of the Nativity, with a bent old man standing before him: 'Is this everything it seems? You don't belong here'. Even in the icon of the Nativity there is a place for doubt. And then the midwife washing the child—midwives, important, but scarcely noticed. It is an important role in the Church; Socrates saw his role, not as a teacher, but someone who opened up minds by discussion and dialogue,

[2] *Windows*, 1.
[3] This and the following quotations in this paragraph are from *Windows*, 7–10.

helping thoughts to come to birth—a kind of midwife, his role 'maieutic'. Then the shepherds, representing nature; the magi, culture; the angels, watching over the scene, the animals beside the manger (the 'ox and ass' of Isaiah's prophecy); a tree—and above all, the hand of God from which emerge three rays, symbolizing the Trinity. The cave and the manger are in darkness: the Christ child comes into the darkness of the world; God loves the world by coming to it at its darkest. Wendy quotes the mysterious remark of Evdokimov's: 'Only God can break the infernal MONAD, the oneness of it, from within'.[4]

Next, an icon of the Archangel Raphael,[5] 'the archangel of healing', the 'journeying angel who comes with us and makes ordinary places into places of pilgrimage'—transfiguring the world. So we need to look at the icon in silence, *hesychia*, and in that silence learn to look. Wendy quotes the poet (Theodore) Roethke: 'I have recovered my tenderness through long looking'. A long patient looking, for looking can be aggressive, seeking to seize and possess; Wendy takes an image from falconry, 'hooding the gaze', making the falcon wait. For us 'hooding the gaze' means learning to wait; it is about interiorizing the senses—Wendy recalls the 'story of Baron von Hügel wrapped up in his cloak praying in the Kensington Carmelite church: hooding the gaze and moving into the interiority in which we can wait on God'. The senses—all of them—for Wendy goes on to speak of an inner *listening*, 'listening with the circumcised ear', as it has been called. Then *touch*—a 'sense of presence'; *smell*—a sensitivity to 'what is fragrant and what stinks in the spiritual life, learning discernment'; and *taste*, quoting George Herbert: 'All my sweet sour days, / I will boast, lament, and praise'.[6] It is a theme

---

[4] Unidentified quotation.

[5] *Windows*, 10–13.

[6] I think Wendy must have been quoting from memory. The last verses of 'Bitter-sweet' read: 'And all my sowre-sweet days / I will lament, and love', in *The Works of George Herbert*, ed. F. E. Hutchinson (Oxford: Clarendon Press, 1941), 171.

that Wendy had earlier visited in the Guild of Pastoral Psychology pamphlet she had written with David Holt, on that occasion relating the treatment of the senses explicitly to the Christian Father, St Gregory of Nyssa.[7]

Wendy remarks that '[t]here is about icons a fantastic sense of depth, a sort of distilled suffering. There is no outer source of light in icons, no reflections, no shadows. The inner light is thought to come from behind'. Icons are sometimes called 'praise of God in colour'[8] because

> they give us glimpses of glory and the presence of others who are stilled; they have found that inner stillness of waiting that requires of us both the unknowing of the mind beyond all concepts, and even more difficult sometimes, the undoing of the heart.[9]

Then follow two icons of the Annunciation,[10] which provokes some reflections on the heart, and the way in which the space between the icon and the one who beholds and venerates is sometimes called the 'place of the heart', which leads Wendy into a meditation of what the annunciation says to us: things like —

> 'Wake up', 'Be watchful', 'I sleep but my heart wakes', and one becomes *disponible*, available, able to put oneself at the disposal of truth. Can we be self emptying, available, receptive, attentive? We have to learn to respond to 'a lifetime of annunciations'. We have to learn, as

---

[7] David Holt and Wendy Robinson, *Dreamwork and Prayer*, Guild of Pastoral Psychology Lecture, 194 (London: Guild of Pastoral Psychology, 1978), 37–40.

[8] Attributed to Evgeny Trubetskoy, Russian would-be émigré, who died of typhus just before embarking on the ship leaving Novorossiysk with the remnant of the White Army in 1920. Wendy is referring to his essays on icons, published in French translation: Eugène Troubetzkoï, *Trois Études sur l'icône* (Paris: YMCA-Press/O.E.I.L., 1986); there is an English translation in Eugene Trubetskoi, *Icons: Theology in Colour* (Crestwood NY: St Vladimir's Seminary Press, 1973), the first of which is called in the original Russian, Умозрение в красках — 'Contemplation in colours'.

[9] *Windows*, 12–13.

[10] Idem, 13–15.

T. S. Eliot said in *Four Quartets*: 'The bone's prayer to Death its God. Only the hardly, barely prayable / Prayer of the one Annunciation.'[11]

Then the icon of the Sign—with the arms of the Mother of God raised in prayer, while Christ appears in a mandorla between her hands, presumably as in the womb (a point Wendy surprisingly misses), as the 'sign' is the sign of Isaiah 7:14–15, the sign, refused by the King, but nevertheless given by Isaiah, of a 'virgin who shall conceive and bear a son'.[12]

Then two icons of the Child and Mother (as Wendy put it in *Windows for the Soul*): an icon of the Mother of God holding the Christ child, and the icon of the Dormition of the Mother of God, in which Christ cradles her soul, in the form of a child, before taking the soul up into heaven—her death or falling asleep, κοίμησις or dormition— an earnest of the transfer (μετάστασις) of her body into heaven. The two icons together portray 'the joyful and suffering shape of a lifetime and a deathtime'.[13]

The next two icons are further icons of Mother and Child, the *Eleousa*, 'of loving tender mercy', and the *Hodigitria*, in which the Mother of God points to her son as the eternal way (*hodos*). Wendy remarks (in a variant of a phrase already encountered) that Mary 'is

---

[11] Possibly a half-memory of 'a lifetime's death in love' (T. S. Eliot, *The Dry Salvages*, V), drawn to 'annunciations' by the quotation in the next sentence. There are, however, two other mentions of 'annunciation' in *The Dry Salvages*, II: 'the unprayable / Prayer at the calamitous annunciation', 'the undeniable / Clamour of the bell of the last annunciation'. Perhaps this gave Wendy the idea of annunciations, in the plural. She returns to seeing annunciation in terms of 'a lifetime's death in love' a few years later in her contribution to Metropolitan Kallistos' *Festschrift*, discussed below. The Eliot is from *The Dry Salvages*, II. (The transcription has been corrected. As with some other pieces, Wendy's talk was evidently recorded and then transcribed, with inevitable errors. It seems that Wendy had not checked the transcript.)

[12] The Greeks know this icon as the *Platētera*—Πλατητέρα τῶν οὐρανῶν, 'wider than the heavens'—for Mary contained in her womb one who himself contains the heavens.

[13] *Windows*, 16; again alluding to Eliot.

not so much an object of faith as the foundation of our Hope, the flower and fruit ripened in worship and tradition'.[14]

Then follow a metal icon of the Cross and the icon of the Resurrection, the *Anastasis*. Wendy's comments are very brief: 'Let us pray that Christ will pull us out of the hells that we humans can create'.[15]

And then, finally, the famous icon of the Trinity by the monk-iconographer St Andrey Rublev, with a somewhat inaccurate account of the cleaning of the icon—not in Marxist Russia, but before the Revolution, as it was a centrepiece of an exhibition in Moscow in 1912. On the 'reverse perspective' of the icon, Wendy comments

> The lines of the table are coming outwards, not going inwards to a vanishing point so that the cup is seen half way towards us, slanted towards us, at the centre of the universe. The figures seem profoundly beyond masculine and feminine. At the same time Neither and Both! The Icon represents the Trinity, united yet not confused, distinct yet not divided, and always mysterious.[16]

To summarize, one might say that Wendy's introduction to the icon is primarily an introduction to prayer. She does not say much about 'praying with icons', I think wisely, for when people ask me about how to pray with icons, I have a sense that they think there is some technique that they need to learn. However, as one reads what she has to say (one should remember that, after presenting each icon, there was a period of silence), the central notions of prayer—the heart, silence, attention, an involvement of the body through (paradoxically) spiritualized, or interiorized, senses—are dwelt upon.

---

[14] *Windows*, 17–18.

[15] Idem, 18.

[16] Section on the Trinity Icon: Idem, 19–22.

5
INTERLUDE: DARKNESS AND DEPRESSION

To close this section on Faith and Orthodoxy, before going on to talk about the other 'partner' in the difficult marriage that made an 'honest woman' out of Wendy, I want to discuss briefly the pamphlet Canon Gonville ffrench-Beytagh, to which Wendy contributed an epilogue, *Out of the Depths: Encountering Depression.* It seems to me this is not inappropriate here, for, after all, it was ffrench-Beytagh who introduced Wendy to the Jesus Prayer. The pamphlet is primarily a text by ffrench-Beytagh about his own frequent and disabling experiences of depression, and what helped him to find his way out—especially the psalms which remained with him during his depressions as part of his daily reading, morning and evening, of the Anglican Divine Office. From what ffrench-Beytagh says, the kind of help he found in the Psalms and the Office was not so much their meaning, but their resonances—what the sounds evoked, even what they felt like in his mouth, as he said them. As he says,

> Even the great depths of Psalm 130, the *de profundis* psalm, do not really mean much to me; although the Latin words *de profundis* ('out of the depths') do, simply because they are low in sound and reverberate rather like the notes on a cello, one of the few kinds of music that can reach me.[1]

Later on he speaks in similar terms of phrases from the Psalms: 'that phrase, "multitude of mercy" [Ps. 69:17] makes a lovely deep sound

---

[1] Gonville ffrench-Beytagh, *Out of the Depths: Encountering Depression,* epilogue by Wendy Robinson, Fairacres Publications 162 (Oxford: SLG Press, 1990; 2nd edn, 2010), 2.

and is repeated elsewhere in the Psalms, e. g. Ps. 5:7 and Ps. 51:1'.[2]
Sometimes just part of a phrase seemed to want to be reclaimed:

> There came a day when I wanted to reclaim Psalm 37:32: 'The law
> of his God is in his heart: and his goings shall not slide.' The law of
> God had at one time been in my heart, but latterly it had just been
> in my memory, and I very much wanted not just to be obedient, but
> to have that true obedience springing from my heart again.[3]

But we are concerned first of all with Wendy, so let us turn to
her epilogue. She begins with a quotation from Romano Guardini:

> Melancholy is too painful, it reaches too deeply into the roots of
> human existence to permit us to leave it to the psychiatrists ... We
> believe there is a question here of something closely related to the
> depths of human nature...[4]

My first reaction is to wonder how close depression really is to
melancholy, but without Wendy to ask, that is a digression. There are
several points Wendy picks up from ffrench-Beytagh's paper. First,
depression has to do with *moods*:

> As the mood deepens, feelings, sensations (often with a bodily com-
> ponent) of emptiness, darkness, tiredness, inertia, capitulation grow
> into a state of bleak, dreary helplessness and hopelessness.[5]

Wendy suggests that the meaning of feelings, moods, need to be
taken more seriously by theologians:

> The tradition shies away from their inconstancy. Yet moods recur.
> They are constant in their inconstancy and are indicators of where
> we are, how we are, who we are, in relation to our own embodied
> being, to our being in the body of our social world and in the Body
> of Christ. Moods are about states of being that are common to all

---

[2] ffrench-Beytagh, *Out of the Depths*, 5.

[3] Idem, 6.

[4] Romano Guardini, 'The Meaning of Melancholy', in *The Focus of Freedom*
(Dublin: Helicon, 1966), 55, quoted in *Out of the Depths*, 17.

[5] ffrench-Beytagh, *Out of the Depths*, 19–20.

human experience and have, therefore, deep meaning and significance in our relation to God and to each other.[6]

Sometimes moods are a reaction to loss, or bereavement. We need, Wendy urges, to develop a more adequate theology of what a viable self-love and self-respect are about: they are about the interaction between love of God, love of neighbour, love of self; for, she remarks, 'you cannot give away, or sacrifice, what you never had in the first place'.[7] A point she gleans from Liberation theology is the need to stop our identifying with the 'victim-self in our experience'. And finally Wendy suggests that the '[e]xperience of darkness, depression, dereliction are so much part of maturing into the depths of friendship with God'. Some of this might sound like the importance of self-esteem, and the need to cultivate this. But elsewhere Wendy seems to warn against this:

> We have come in the West to decry the emphasis in some kinds of theology on being humble wretched sinners, more concerned with suffering and self-imposed crosses, but as I get older I am more sure about starting there. Where else? As a sinner. 'Here I am, Lord. What a mess!'[8]

---

[6] ffrench-Beytagh, *Out of the Depths*, 19.

[7] This and the following quotations in this paragraph are from ffrench-Beytagh, *Out of the Depths*, 21–2.

[8] 'Journey', 15.

6
DEPTH PSYCHOLOGY

The other side of the marriage that Wendy felt made an 'honest woman' of her was her practice of depth psychology. From starting as a teacher (her first post was at what was then called an 'Approved School' for difficult or delinquent teenage girls), Wendy soon acquired qualifications in psychiatric social work, studying with D. W. Winnicott and attending lectures by the then (and maybe still) controversial R. D. Laing. By the time of her return from South Africa, initially to Oxford where she spent nearly 25 years (from 1967 to 1991), a long period of comparative stability, she began to style herself as a 'Jungian psychotherapist'. However, at one point (I suspect in the late-1980s, or even the 1990s), when I asked her about her psychological 'allegiance', she mentioned her Jungian training, but said that, like most practising psychotherapists, she was eclectic. The longer Wendy felt herself having been made an 'honest woman', the harder it seems (or I have found) to locate her own psychological position. She was very well read (one feature of our friendship was her attempt to get me to read more widely in American poetry and criticism—her own sympathies and reading constantly surprised me) and had a good (though often inaccurate) memory; she readily drew on ideas that had attracted her, wherever they came from. Nonetheless, she could sometimes give a straightforward account of the Jungian position; an example of this is her brief contribution to the 2009 Conference of the Association of Orthodox Christian Psychotherapists on 'The Ground of Our Being: A Study of Hidden Consciousness'. As I have mentioned, it is indeed brief—four pages—and somewhat schematic:[1] after a couple of pages of introduction, the 'layers' of the psyche, according to Jung, are laid out with a diagram and a few, extremely penetrating, notes. Her introductory comments begin with the felt need, especially in relation to religion, for depth: religion is felt to be 'shallow', simply reflecting a sense that 'culturally and socially' the way we live seems 'unbearably shallow'. She quotes the poet, Richard Wilbur:

> All that we do
> Is touched with ocean, yet we remain
> On the shore of what we know.[2]

She has a few words on Freud, and recommends two books: David Bakan's *Freud and the Jewish Mystical Tradition* and 'Paul Ricoeur's essential study', *Freud and Philosophy*. She then turns to Jung, mentioning his autobiographical *Memories, Dreams, Reflections*—a 'gripping read for our times', and rather testily rebukes those Orthodox who dismiss his thought as 'mere Gnosticism'.

I think I am trying to clarify in my own mind where Wendy was 'coming from', as we say, as a psychotherapist, and what seems to be emerging is this: Jungian analytical psychology was certainly important to her. Other labels she employs are 'depth psychology' and 'psychodynamic', both of which belong in the same fold, so to speak, and convey a concern to reach beyond behaviour and analyse the hidden, even unconscious, roots of our behaviour, and achieve healing through enabling self-examination and self-understanding.

---

[1] 'The Ground of our Being: A Study of Hidden Consciousness', Paper delivered at the conference of the Association of Orthodox Christian Psychotherapists, (2009), 10–13.
[2] 'For Dudley', in Richard Wilbur, *Collected Poems 1943–2004* (New York: Harcourt, Inc., 2004), 211.

7
THE NOTION OF THE ONTOLOGICAL

One notion to which Wendy returns again and again is that of the ontological. We have already encountered this when I discussed the second occasion where she talked of being made an 'honest woman': in the article published in the journal *Psychodynamic Counselling* called 'The Quest for the Heart of the Work', with the significant subtitle, 'An Ontological Approach to Spirituality and Psychotherapy/ Counselling'. There she says that the term ontology offered itself as signalling 'sustained attention to the mystery of being and human being': that phrase, *mystery of being and human being*, could be rendered in German as 'das Geheimnis des Seins und des Daseins', and as such sounds very reminiscent of Heidegger. I don't know whether Wendy read Heidegger (though it would not surprise me), but I have not come across any reference to him in her writings. Heidegger was, and still is, in the air, as it were, and echoes of him in attempts to understand how we stand in relation to the world in which we live—the world of nature and of people—would hardly be surprising. But it does not seem to me a road down which we should go. Much of Wendy's reflection on ontology, in this sense, seems to arise from work that she did, and papers that she wrote, in conjunction with David Holt, a 'Jungian analytical psychologist', as she describes him.[1] There are two pieces among the material I have been working with that witness to this collaboration—*Dreamwork and Prayer* and *Pastoral Counselling: An Exercise in Ontology*—the former a Guild Lecture of the Guild of Pastoral Psychology,[2] and the latter the report written by

---

[1] 'Quest', 20.

David Holt and Wendy summarizing the results of a study group, led by them, between September 1977 and June 1979.[3] The Guild Lecture seems to have consisted of two complementary lectures, one by David, the other by Wendy, which seem to have been given in 1978, at the mid-point of the study group that produced *Pastoral Counselling*, the report that is the joint work of David and Wendy. Alas, I can make little or nothing of David's ideas, though it is clear that Wendy valued his work highly. That also means that I don't know where I am in the report, *Pastoral Counselling*: I pick up ideas that seem familiar, but for the most part I am at sea. I shall therefore discuss briefly Wendy's article, 'The Quest for the Heart of the Work', and her contribution to the Guild lecture, 'Dreamwork and Prayer', starting with the earlier piece, the Guild Lecture of 1978.

There are so many ideas in Wendy's 'Dream-Work and the Work of Prayer' (the title of her contribution) that it is extremely difficult to summarize, and many of these take the form of (anonymized) stories from her therapeutic practice. She begins by drawing attention to something that both depth psychology and the world of faith seem to acknowledge they have in common:

> Both of them were trying to explore and express what IS and I began to feel that the hiatus between them, if they tried to speak and hear each other, was a reflection of the hesitation: the wonder, awe, fear, the catch of the breath, that we all feel at times, in the presence of what IS.[4]

I don't think Wendy uses the term 'ontology' in this lecture, but this remark makes it clear that the realm of the ontological was already a concern for Wendy: a sense of the IS, before which we feel awe, wonder, disquiet. Wendy then moves directly to engage with

---

[2] *Dreamwork and Prayer*, Guild of Pastoral Psychology Lecture, no. 194 (London: Guild of Pastoral Psychology, 1978).

[3] David Holt and Wendy Robinson, *Pastoral Counselling: An Exercise in Ontology* (Oxford: ZiPrint, 1980), 90 pp.

[4] *Dreamwork*, 26.

Ricoeur, and his book *Freud and Philosophy*, taking from him a series of oppositions: Reduction of illusion ~ restoration or recollection of meaning/amounting to a *call*; Willingness to suspect ~ willingness to listen; Vow of rigour ~ vow of obedience—and with these oppositions, the need for discrimination. The question Ricoeur seems to be putting to Freud is whether, with his hermeneutic of suspicion, he is not reductionist in his view of the world. 'Does not this discipline of the real, this ascesis of the necessary, lack the grace of imagination, the upsurge of the possible?',[5] so that the constraint of the necessary, of *Anankē*, is reduced to something anonymous and impersonal, leading to a 'world shorn of God'.[6] If we listen to the 'grace of imagination', there may open up a sense of Presence, that expresses the heart of all that we mean by 'personal': the Love of Creation. Wendy continues from her summary of Ricoeur:

> Necessity and Love both bind us, in different ways. To move between them rigorously, obediently, gracefully is a lifetime's work: perhaps more than a lifetime … Perhaps more than anything the Turning (the Teshuvah, metanoia) will help us: the ability to say I am sorry; I will start again. The longest journey, as the proverb says, begins with the next step.[7]

To unpack all that would be a task indeed—and a tribute to the depth of Wendy's insight.

Wendy continues by relating the story from Daniel of Nebuchadnezzar's dream—a dream that he didn't so much have, as it had him: it kept recurring, and he knew it was the same dream, but he could never remember it. Wendy's discussion is lengthy, but her conclusion is concise: 'Perhaps he too [the author, I think] sensed the presence of a forgotten dream, full of a latent potentiality, that stood

---

[5] Paul Ricoeur, *Freud and Philosophy*, trans. Denis Savage (New Haven: Yale University Press, 1970), 36.

[6] Wendy paraphrases Ricoeur's 'world shorn of the God of faith', Ricoeur, *Freud and Philosophy*, 327.

[7] *Dreamwork*, 27.

in need of remembering and interpretation'[8]—which leads her into a discussion of the way in which prayer reaches out beyond our comprehension, and the dream, sometimes, reaches back from the beyond into our consciousness—something in which our desire, both the desire we are aware of and that which seems to well up from hidden depths, finds expression. Wendy moves on, via a discussion of Gregory of Nyssa's understanding of the spiritualization of the senses, as an aspect of prayer, not dissimilar to what we found above in her discussion of the icon of the Archangel Raphael in *Windows for the Soul*. She then returns to her engagement with Ricoeur's criticism of Freud, and concludes in poetic vein:

> The CENTRE, of the model, the turning-point of intersection: is it then the place of conjugation between Necessity and Love, where illusion can be reduced and meaning restored by participation in faith, in hope, in love, which live between man and man, between God and all Creation? Can I hear a Call, feel the pull of that Centre? It sounds both far and near. Is it a dream that I shall forget on waking to reality? Or is it the Supreme Reality that remembers me, draws me, calls me to dream and to pray, so that I may not altogether forget the Ground of my being and that I may remember the Love of Creation?[9]

Although 'ontology' is not mentioned in this paper, it seems to me that in unfolding her ideas Wendy introduces us to a feeling, a sense of presence—presence before what IS, or even one whose essence is simply IS-ness: for ontology is the study of what is, of being. One can hardly read this without recalling, as a kind of Aeolian echo,[10] the way in which God reveals his name in the version of the Bible read in the Orthodox Church (the Greek Septuagint): 'I am the one who IS' (ὁ ὤν: Exod. 3:14).

---

[8] *Dreamwork*, 30.

[9] Idem, 42.

[10] An idea stolen, without apology, from Murray Cox and Alice Theilgaard, *Mutative Metaphors in Psychotherapy: The Aeolian Mode* (London: Jessica Kingsley Publishers, 2nd edn 1997). I heard more Aeolian echoes reading Wendy's pieces for this essay than ever before.

If 'ontology' is not mentioned in the Guild Lecture of 1978, it is the ostensible subject of her article, published 20 years later, 'The Quest for the Heart of the Work'. Nevertheless, despite the prominence of the notion of ontology, what Wendy has to say about it is revealed glancingly, tangentially. Like another of her papers, this paper was accompanied by visual aids, to be precise, stones (the other paper is called 'Sounding Stones'), the first stone of which (the 'Central Stone') is a stone with a hole in it, 'rather like a Barbara Hepworth sculpture', as Wendy says.[11] (A present Wendy once gave me was a small stone with a hole in it that had been sculpted by her husband, Edward, to form a kind of three-dimensional 'Moebius Strip'—from any point on which, one could reach any other point, without crossing an edge.) This stone, placed at the centre, is to convey the sense that 'at the heart of our work there will always be a sense of mystery, of the unknown-yet-present, a sense of wonder at Being', and she goes on to quote the words on Paul Klee's tombstone: 'Somewhat nearer than usual to the heart of creation but still too far away'.

The first stone (after the central one) introduces an idea Wendy returns to in other papers: what she calls here 'the danger of ontological collapse'—the danger of bracketing out any sense that 'prayer, contemplation, meditation and wise silence' (all of which are forms of attention that 'let be') have any place in the human condition and in seeking to meet human needs when things have gone wrong.

> There are forms of attention [like those listed] that can honour the sense of Presence (of the Divine) on which life itself and the soul depend for their very existence ... If we fail to attend to the mystery at the heart of things, then we stand in danger of ontological collapse.[12]

—leaving other forms of being—social structures, the marriage, family, relationships, children and individual lives—to be 'burdened with weights of meaning that they cannot carry without danger of collapse'.[13]

---

[11] This and the next quotation in this paragraph are from 'Quest', 21.

[12] 'Quest', 23.

[13] Idem, 24.

Stone Two concerns the 'history of desire', for 'ontology reminds me that desire has a teleological, a purposive pull towards its own transcendence, as it responds to a call that is beyond all forms of immediacy'. If lack is the beginning of desire, then it is endless, because desire is, in the end, desire for God, the Divine, the Eternal Thou. Here as with the first stone, there is the need to 'let be', by forms of attention that allow the other to be, rather than seeking to possess. We need, Wendy counsels, to attend to the experience of women mystics and their

> experiences of the divine [expressed] in daring and often dizzying erotic language. Attention to them can bring a refreshing glimpse of lands of far distances to be explored which can change our more confined struggles with addictions and compulsions involved in the demands ... [placed] upon an all-too-human other. Ontological collapse in the realm of 'the history of desire' has a devastating effect.[14]

Stone Three follows on from the second stone, for if there is a history of desire, then this is contained within what Wendy calls 'the mystery of origins and ends' which opens up 'the beyond in our midst', which escapes psychotherapy's 'obsession with origins and theories based on the aetiological causality of adult ills in early childhood'. To get rid of this obsession with an 'archaeological horizon', as a result of which 'we stand in danger of occluding the many areas of human experience that need a teleological, purposive horizon to give them their due value in making for mature adulthood', or at least to diminish it, Wendy refers to Ernest Becker's *The Denial of Death* (1973), in which he argues that 'death ... makes us question ... our *causa sui* project, our assumption that we are in control and do not need God'. Still more compellingly, the prospect of death reminds us forcibly of our 'sense of finitude', which 'opens up unknown levels of being'.[15] In this connection, Wendy refers to a comment of David Holt's on 'the ontological status of accident' —

---

[14] 'Quest', 25.
[15] Idem, 26.

accident that, by definition, we cannot predict, nor factor into our project of control of our lives. She comments: 'Life is too mysterious, and often much too painful, as it carries its shadow of finitude to be treated thus. The why and the how of things does not always equal the what. That things are just the way they are is the more mysterious—and demanding'.[16]

Stone Four—'Paradigm shifts'—seemed to me to be perhaps too much caught up in professional musings about the current (or then current) state of psychotherapy, as it has moved from its roots as a critique of authoritarian structures to acquiescence in a prevailing individualism and concern for the self, together with some disappointment expressed by Wendy over psychotherapy losing contact with its radical roots. Something of the same is the case, too, with Stone Five—'hermeneutics'—in which, nevertheless, Wendy gives a very succinct account of the hermeneutical endeavour:

> Our very being, the world in which we find ourselves—these are not transparent but opaque, full of the unknown and the hidden which we have to seek to find. The very nature of human reflective consciousness means that we have to indwell 'being' and 'the world' to try to interpret their meanings, even as we participate in them.[17]

The 'ontological' turns out, in Wendy's interpretation, to be more directly concerned with interpreting our experience, both in our own lives and in counselling, where the 'hermeneutical circle' could be regarded as defining a space that includes both the counsellor and those seeking counsel, whether as individuals or participating in a group.

I would like to pursue this notion of the ontological a little further, and two leads occur to me to help us on the way. The first is an article I read many years ago by the late Professor Dorothy Emmet (1904–2000) which explored what might be meant by Paul Tillich's

---

[16] 'Quest', 27.
[17] Idem, 30.

notion of the 'Ground of Being',[18] which appeared in *Journal of Theological Studies* in 1964.[19] By this time, Emmet, who at one time had been interested in A. N. Whitehead and process philosophy, had very much come to belong to the dominant Anglo-Saxon philosophical tradition of analytical philosophy, and most of the article consists of a careful, if baffled, exploration of what Tillich could possibly mean in terms of such philosophy. Towards the end of the article, she changes direction, and suggests that the notion of 'Ground of Being' might be understood as 'a metaphysical extension of depth psychology'.[20] Such a view suggests that 'the depths of the human psyche are crude, formless energies', found in both Freud's and Jung's rather different notions of the unconscious, though in Tillich's case it is rather Fromm's influence that is to be detected, 'who allows a person more positive powers than Freud does, not only to accept and understand himself, but also to love and create freely through this acceptance'. Emmet goes on to suggest that Tillich's 'courage to be' comes close to this; she finds him 'illuminating when he cashes what he has to say about the "power of being" in terms of courage overcoming anxiety and the basic fears of meaninglessness which haunt people'. She notes the 'normative significance' Tillich puts on 'the notions of being and non-being', and sees Tillich as speaking of the 'Ground of Being as power mastering formless "non-being"'. Towards the end of the article Emmet suggests that Tillich's 'positive faith is put better by the term "power" rather than "ground of being"'. Reading depth psychology in 'metaphysical' or ontological terms might be a helpful way

---

[18] This notion is alluded to in the title of one of the conferences of the Association of Orthodox Christian Psychotherapists to which Wendy contributed: 'The Ground of our Being: A Study of Hidden Consciousness' (2009), although Wendy did not use the expression in her paper, which was called 'The "Unconscious"'.

[19] Dorothy Emmet, '"The Ground of Being"', *Journal of Theological Studies* NS 15/2 (1964), 280–92, doi.org/10.1093/jts/XV.2.280 (accessed 24 January 2024).

[20] This and the following quotations from Emmet in this paragraph are from 'The Ground of Being', 290–2.

of making sense of Wendy's appeal to the ontological; it would be a way of seeing depth psychological analysis as exploring the ways of being that underlie what it is to be human.

That is one lead. The other is the prevalence of the notion of the 'ontological' in much Orthodox spirituality. One of the motives behind this is a sense that in our encounter with God in Christ what happens is not just a matter of a change in behaviour or outlook on life, but something much deeper that reaches to the very core, or depths, of our being—a transformation that is veritably 'ontological'. So, for example, in his book on the spiritual vision of his great-uncle, St Sophrony of Essex, Fr Nikolai sums up what St Sophrony is saying in the first chapter of *We Shall See Him as He Is* thus:

> As a response to human initiative, to an intellectual quest, man experiences an 'ontological' change with his perception of self, characterized by the 'feeling' of the 'futility of any and every acquisition on earth'.[21]

I think that part of the reason for the use in this context of the 'ontological' is that in the human engagement with God, the human is encountering his Creator; it is not an engagement between other creatures, as in personal relationships, it is engagement with the One to whom we owe our being—and that cannot leave our being unaltered. I don't think this should be dismissed (as Rowan Williams did in an early essay) as an attempt 'to safeguard a view of participation-in-God, *theosis*, which seems insupportably "realist"';[22] it is rather an attempt to take seriously the divine dimension of a 'personal' relationship with God. St Sophrony's concern for being, *bytie*, has been

---

[21] Nicholas V. Sakharov, *I Love, Therefore I Am: The Theological Legacy of Archimandrite Sophrony* (Crestwood, NY: SVSP, 2002), 230, referring to the first chapter of St Sophrony's *We Shall See Him as He Is* (Tolleshunt Knights, Essex: Stavropegic Monastery of St John the Baptist, 1988), 'The Grace of Mindfulness of Death', 10–18.

[22] Rowan D. Williams, 'The Philosophical Structures of Palamism', in *Eastern Churches Review* 9 (1977), 27–44, here 44.

traced back to his early experiences as an artist in Paris in the 1920s, where the Russian term, *Bytie,* was used to designate a group of Russian artists working there by capturing the nature of their understanding of art as less depiction, but rather as re-creation in one medium or another of the being or essence of the subject of the painting, sculpture, or other artwork (an understanding of art close to that embraced by David Jones around the same time).

These leads do not explain, still less explain away, the importance of the ontological to Wendy. Looking back over what I have said, it strikes me that the term 'ontological' earns its place in the term Wendy uses, 'ontological collapse'—the result, in human life, of trying to sustain structures of being and living, that need ultimately to be rooted in an encounter with God, by merely human structures, which in the nature of things cannot bear the weight of what is required of them, for the 'ontological' needs to be rooted in the divine, however imperfectly glimpsed.

8
TOWARDS A THEOLOGY FOR PSYCHOTHERAPISTS

Many of the ideas we have been encountering as we explore the primarily psychological or psychotherapeutic side of Wendy's thought are found again in a pamphlet of the Oxford Christian Institute for Counselling recording a talk Wendy gave at a one-day consultation in Oxford in October 1994—a little earlier than the article we have just been exploring. It is called 'The Lost Traveller's Dream: Developing a Theology for Working with Mental Illness.'[1] Wendy begins by lamenting that after nearly forty years of counselling and badgering theologians to do something about providing an adequate theology for those engaged in mental health, there has been little response, so it has been left for her to sketch out such a theology.[2] The first theme introduced is that traditional theology *makes too much noise*; we need to move from noise to silence. This noise, she suggests, has to do with our ticklishness about our presuppositions, quoting the still-neglected philosopher, R. G. Collingwood:[3] ticklishness that can make one laugh, but also be extremely painful, and quite sadistic

---

[1] In *Cosmos, Crisis & Christ*, 35–48.
[2] An obvious exception to this complaint might be Jean-Claude Larchet, for whom some such endeavour, alongside his more professional concern with St Maximos the Confessor, has been a constant concern: such works as *Thérapeutique des maladies spirituelles* (3rd edn, rev. and corr., Paris: Cerf, 1997); *L'inconscient spirituel* (Paris: Cerf, 2008); and *Théologie du corps* (Paris: Cerf, 2009).
[3] R. G. Collingwood, *An Essay on Metaphysics* (Oxford: Clarendon Press, 1940), 131.

in the end. This leads Wendy to consider 'borderlands', that become especially noticeable when we are talking with one another across different disciplines, for we are constantly being drawn out of our own comfort zones, and need to learn to

> thrive not on theoretical or theological certainties, but on the crackle and twang of ambiguities, *un*certainties, on a tension pulled to the pitch of crucifixion in some people's lives, if we are to honour both the poetry and the prose, the prosaicness of suffering, the pain, the *power* of lives lived.[4]

This also leads Wendy to refer to, without actually quoting, a remark of the French philosopher Gaston Bachelard, that the image touches the *depth* before it stirs the *surface:*[5] a citation that forms a kind of *Leitmotiv* in Cox and Theilgaard's *Mutative Metaphors in Psychotherapy*, to which Wendy does not refer here, but does elsewhere, which I think she must have read with a sense of recognition, for she herself is always probing metaphors in her analysis of the psyche.[6] The concept of borderlands leads to another metaphor of great significance to Wendy, the 'beyond in our midst', with the corollary that 'between the edges of our existence and the centre, there is a special trajectory of desire, or longing' — that 'history of desire' that is itself a corollary of the notion of ontology. All these states and experiences are illustrated from everyday experience as well as from the terrible experiences of some of those she has counselled. Of these latter, Wendy tells us,

> They remain for us uncomfortable, sometimes uncouth pilgrims of the absolute, victims of a sort of nihilism that can lie at the heart of

---

[4] 'Lost Traveller's Dream', 36.

[5] 'Mais l'image a touché les profondeurs avant d'émouvoir la surface': in Gaston Bachelard, *La poétique de l'espace* (12th edn: Paris: Quadrige/PUF, 1984; first edition, 1957), 7.

[6] In the bibliography to Wendy's contribution, 'From Metaphor to Symbol in Creative Writing', to the 2011 conference of the Association of Orthodox Christian Psychotherapists on 'Symbols and Symbolism': Conference Proceedings, 12 (privately published pamphlet). Wendy's contribution is on pp. 3–12.

our societies. What we have to do is to witness, witness, witness what they share with us about how things are, before God and others, and not pretend it is otherwise.[7]

Boundary riders, prophets among the afflicted, survival skills: these are other themes around which Wendy's thoughts are woven. 'Borderlands, boundaries, edges are places of terror and devastation, and also places of rare, even unique, shy, heart-rending beauty'.[8] She cites David Jones on the *genius loci*, the spirit of each place, who is 'a rare one for locality',[9] and a little later cites a passage from the same poem, to which she will return to dwell on at length, about the need to learn 'to laugh in the mantle of variety'.[10]

How do we find Christ in such places? We have to 'turn to the body', as God did in the Incarnation. 'Our task is to help people "to bear the beams of Love" instead of to escape from them into some terrible form of suffering'.[11] With such a love, we are tempted to maintain 'theologically' from what we know about the Gospel and about Christ 'that compassion for affliction is easy. It is not.'[12] Wendy quotes Simone Weil, 'It repels, rather than attracts.'

Deep, gaping wounds repel rather than attract … The terrible wounds of the afflicted with whom we work awaken our wounds,

---

7 'Lost Traveller's Dream', 40. *The Pilgrim of the Absolute* is the title of a collection of the writings of Léon Bloy (1846–1917), selected and edited by Raïssa Maritain (New York: Pantheon, 1947).

8 'Lost Traveller's Dream', 40.

9 'Lost Traveller's Dream', 42, referring to 'The Tutelar of the Place', in David Jones, *The Sleeping Lord and Other Fragments* (London: Faber and Faber, 1974), 59.

10 'Lost Traveller's Dream', 43.

11 Ibid., quoting William Blake's 'The Little Black Boy' from *Songs of Innocence*, in *The Poetry and Prose of William Blake*, ed. Geoffrey Keynes (London: The Nonesuch Press, 1946), 54.

12 'Lost Traveller's Dream', 44. It is perhaps worth noting here the close parallel to this in 'The Love of God and Affliction': 'Thus compassion for the afflicted is an impossibility', in Simone Weil, *Waiting on God* (London: Routledge and Kegan Paul Ltd, 1951), 65.

our unmet needs, the things that have gone wrong for us too, so that we have to learn to look to our own knowledge, our own healing, in order to be able to stay close to the deep wounds of the really afflicted. And we have to learn what it means to 'wait on God'.[13]

Bridge builders—Finding God—Living with doubt: leading to reflection of 'The place between', where we have to wait … and guard against 'ontological collapse'. Her reflections end with a quotation from William Blake, which contains the title of her paper:

> Tho' thou art Worship'd by the Names Divine
> Of Jesus & Jehovah, thou art still
> The Sun of Morn in weary Night's decline,
> The lost Traveller's Dream under the Hill.[14]

We have just followed Wendy's attempt to construct the kind of theology needed by those who seek to meet people at the extremities of existence: a call that might come to any of us who seek to follow the crucified Christ, but for some has become in itself a way of life. So this section on 'depth psychology', as one of the poles of Wendy's own vocation, ends with her own attempt to think through the tension between her professional vocation as an analyst and her life of faith. In the final section of this reflection I want to look at two areas of her thought that can only, in my view, be considered by taking into account the marriage of ways of life and thought that made an 'honest woman' of her.

---

[13] 'Lost Traveller's Dream', 44. Wendy's original reference is 'Simone Weil, *Waiting on God*, Routledge, London, 1951, pp. 63–8', but I cannot find it on these pages, which belong to the paper, 'The love of God and Affliction' (pp. 63–78), though it could be regarded as a summary of pp. 64–7.

[14] From the epilogue to 'From the Sexes: The Gates of Paradise', in *Blake*, ed. Keynes, p. 579 (text corrected against Keynes' edition).

9
THE UNION OF MIND AND HEART

In this penultimate section I want to look at two pamphlets first issued as Fairacres Publications: 'Sounding Stones: Reflections on the Mystery of the Feminine', and 'Exploring Silence'—both essays exploring themes very important to Wendy.[1] (It occurs to me that taking together the themes of silence and women might call to mind 1 Cor. 14:34—but that association of ideas is far from what we are embarking on now.)

Wendy was very conscious of the lack of space/place given to women in the Christian churches, although in many churches more and more has been done to remedy this (at least apparently), and she was especially conscious of what one might call the invisible presence of women in the Orthodox Churches, manifest as a bleak absence in positions of power and authority. I remember her commenting that she could hardly be expected to feel represented in a Church in which all authority and decision-making seemed to be exercised by men with beards and black hats. Early on in her life, she had learnt from the Quakers about 'speaking truth to power', but she had also learnt that the life of institutions dwarfs that of men and women—they 'will go on long after we are dead, and … reforming zeal needs to find a small focus, and throw energy into working at that, and not thinking one can change everything'.[2] One might think that the ordination of women to the priesthood might well constitute such a 'small focus' for her, but I am not at all sure Wendy would

---

[1] Fairacres Publications 99 (1987) and 170 (2013); the latter was originally published in 1974 as Fairacres Publications 36. References here are to the edition in *Cosmos, Crisis & Christ*.

[2] 'Journey', 3.

have accepted that; nevertheless, her long-term witness—both by what she said and, even more, by what she did, what she *was*—to what women could contribute to the Orthodox Church (a contribution at present denied them or at least heavily qualified) had an influence on the attitude of many to such questions, even hierarchs whose opinions are widely known and respected.

What Wendy wrote on the question of the feminine in itself and in the Church is mainly confined (so far as I am aware) to the essay, 'Sounding Stones', mentioned above, and what I have found there is confirmed by my memory of conversations with her (or listened into by me) on the subject. 'The subject': this was rarely directly the question of the ordination of women to the priesthood, but, as in the subtitle of the pamphlet indicates, the wider subject of the place of the feminine— in the Church and in human life. For Wendy was convinced that the feminine has been overlooked and underestimated in patriarchal institutions such as Western society as we know it, and as it has existed for centuries and even millennia, and in the Church, which reflects the society in which it was born, in this way as in others. Wendy belonged to an ecumenical group that met over three years (consisting of five women and five men: two Orthodox, two or three Catholics, one United Reformed, and four or five Anglicans), and published their report, *A Fearful Symmetry: The Complementarity of Men and Women in Ministry*—in a timely way, but not I think deliberately—on the eve of the vote in 1992 of the General Synod of the Church of England in favour of the ordination of women to the priesthood.[3] In that report (to which I shall make some reference, conscious of the fact that signatories to a report are not necessarily in agreement with its every line), it is affirmed from time to time that the period of patriarchy has lasted 4,000 years, and was a change that can thus be dated back to the beginning of the second millennium BC. I can guess whose view is being endorsed by the report, but it seems to me little more than a theory.

---

[3] Bishop Geoffrey Rowell, ed., *A Fearful Symmetry: The Complementarity of Men and Women in Ministry* (London: SPCK, 1992).

Wendy's view was that there is a profound complementarity between the masculine and the feminine, and though this complementarity does not match without remainder on to males and females, nevertheless the neglect of the feminine has been institutionalized, making it difficult even, or perhaps especially, for men in power to attend to the feminine side of their nature. Wendy was well aware, too, that the masculine/feminine divide, as we experience it, is not solely the result of nature, but owes a good deal to cultural influences: the contrast takes different forms in different cultures, and is not something simply 'given' in nature. It is also noticeable that the contrast between the masculine and the feminine matches in many respects the contrast between the left-side and right-side of the brain.[4]

---

[4] On which see Iain McGilchrist, *The Master and his Emissary* (New Haven and London: Yale University Press, 2009) and his *The Matter with Things*, 2 vols. (London: Perspectiva Press, 2021).

10
THE FEMININE

'Sounding Stones: Reflections on the Mystery of the Feminine' is, as the subtitle suggests, concerned not so much with the *contrast* between the masculine and the feminine, as with the feminine itself—the mystery of the feminine. Like 'The Quest for the heart of the work', the talk was illustrated by stones that she had collected 'mostly in the North of England and on Mull and Iona'.[1] She began by placing in the middle a stone with a hole in it (as in the 'Quest') and added stones placed round it in a circle to mark the sections of her talk. The stone symbolizes that 'it's not easy to find words', and she added, 'In the centre I am going to put this stone with a hole in the middle which speaks of the mystery of the feminine, about something silent to which we must be able to hold, and I want to build other stones round it in a circle'. She counsels against 'trying to relate them to each other, just try to take each one and see if it relates to the basic theme for you'.

Wendy begins by quoting from a poem of David Jones, 'The Tutelar of the Place':

> mother of particular perfections
> queen of otherness
> mistress of asymmetry
> patroness of things counter, parti, pied, several
> protectress of things known and handled
> help of things familiar and small
> wardress of the secret crevices
> of things wrapped and hidden
> ...

---

[1] 'Sounding Stones', 50.

arc of differences
tower of individuation
queen of the minivers
laughing in the mantle of variety…[2]

Not just a beautiful prayer to the Mother of God, 'but also something about our feminine need to hold to the "holy diversities"', as Wendy puts it, and she goes on to mention that the feminine is 'most particular', 'dealing with particulars, in small things, in things that matter, that make all the difference', but also, 'on the shadow side, the pernickety bitchiness that's most particular, too particular, too much after each other's guts when something starts to go wrong.'[3] And she continues,

> I think the large inescapable truths are not easily come by in our day and generation, in a time of cultural fragmentation, and the truth, amongst us in the Christian Church too has to be found in bits and pieces, and treasured in the heart when we find it.

She speaks of the need to draw these bits and pieces into our contemplative life, 'to cherish, to treasure, to ponder small things that are given', concluding: 'Now that means that we have to try to learn not to generalize, not to universalize, too soon.' This, however, is what she calls a 'logos capacity', often associated with the masculine, which itself runs the risk of losing 'our own [feminine] sense of the particular'. Furthermore Wendy adds a warning against attempting to

> assimilate or domesticate the truth too much. As women we sometimes have a tendency to want to tame things, to make them domesticated and familiar … but we can go too far. Truths which are large and fierce and not easily approached are turned into tame pussy-cats. They are not! They need to keep their tiger quality.[4]

---

[2] From David Jones, *The Sleeping Lord and Other Fragments* (London: Faber & Faber, 1995), 59–64, here 62–4.

[3] 'Sounding Stones', 51.

[4] Idem, 52.

Let us pause for a moment, and listen to what seem to be 'Aeolian echoes' set off by Wendy's words. Feminine variety contrasted with the masculine 'logos' capacity. First, Enobarbus' comments about Cleopatra's beauty, something Anthony will never forget, and that will prevent him from leaving her, even though at this point it is political madness to stay: 'Age cannot wither her, nor custom stale / Her infinite variety…'. I am inclined to believe that these words were echoing in David Jones's mind, when he wrote the lines Wendy quoted. Cleopatra is, in some ways an archetypal woman, with 'her infinite variety' that she knows fully how to deploy. I thought, too, of Isak Dinesen's understanding of the feminine, for whom 'domestication' never fully conceals the tigerish nature of femininity (I am pretty sure that Wendy introduced me to Isak Dinesen; we certainly had various conversations about her). Or, in a different vein, Paul's reference in Ephesians 3:10 to 'the utterly various wisdom of God' (ἡ πολυποίκιλος σοφία τοῦ Θεοῦ): God's wisdom 'with its intense variety' — wisdom of feminine gender and appearing in the Wisdom literature as God's female companion in creation (Prov. 8:22–31): a counterpart to the masculine *logos*, that Wendy mentions. I wonder if these echoes do not suggest ways in which Wendy's understanding of the feminine might be filled out.

In fact, in Stone 2, Wendy finds a (feminine) companion for *logos* in *eros*, which strikes me as a bit counter-intuitive, as *eros* is of the masculine gender, and as a god, or daemon, appears to be male. She further compares the *logos/eros* complementarity with Jung's pair, *animus/anima* and goes on, through quoting André Louf's notion of 'rocking and chewing the word', to identify a feminine dimension in contemplative prayer. She discusses then problems in the relationship between man and woman: how men often find it difficult to take a woman 'neat', 'not always sure what to do with a woman's strength' — leading to a tendency to find the feminine in weakness, vulnerability, obedience, and submission.[5] And Wendy defends what

---

[5] Cf. 'Sounding Stones', 53.

are often regarded as 'women's wiles', which some women despise. Without practising these wiles, Wendy suggests, women run the risk of making men feel (and be) impotent.

Further stones introduce the idea of a woman's capacity to 'be alone', often made difficult, or frustrated, by a sense of 'the child crying in the night with no language but a cry';[6] what Wendy calls 'stalking our wildness … and to be able to deal with it if it takes us somewhere too far out and up',[7] mentioning in this context the myth of Artemis. On the importance of being 'earthed', she tells us:

> We need repeating, cyclic, rhythmic, ritualistic ways and occupations that can keep us in touch with earth and the deeper cyclic rhythms of the feminine … That capacity is an important part of our life together—feeding the flame slowly, gently, in order not to quench it. And in the Church, being guardians of myth and memory is part of making sure that we are earthed and centred.[8]

In the next section, 'Discovering the creative *No*', she notes:

> something inside us as women which lives in that basic relatedness, needs to be able to say the No in order to let the other be, to save the other from feeling smothered or too tightly bound in our feminine need to give and to love.

Painful, open to being wounded: Wendy notes the close similarity of *blessure* (wound) and *blessing*. And learning 'what the "foot of the Cross" presence with the Beloved in suffering means'.[9] Finally—the last stone— is 'How to Be Near and Far at the Same Time', which means coping with anger, recognizing the danger of masking anger—the need, at times, to make space for a 'fair fight'.

---

[6] 'Sounding Stones', 55 (a somewhat condensed quotation from Tennyson's 'In Memoriam', Section LVI, lines 17–20: 'So runs my dream: but what am I? / An infant crying in the night: / An infant crying for the light: / And with no language but a cry.').

[7] 'Sounding Stones', 57.

[8] Ibid.

[9] Idem, 59.

Wendy concludes by quoting from Simone Weil:

> God created through love and for love. God did not create anything
> except love itself, and the means to love. He created beings capable of
> love from all possible distances. Because no other could do it, he him-
> self went to the greatest possible distance, the infinite distance. This
> infinite distance between God and God, this supreme tearing apart,
> this agony beyond all others, this marvel of love is the crucifixion...
>
> This tearing apart, over which supreme love places the bond of
> supreme union, echoes perpetually across the universe in the midst
> of the silence, like two notes, separate yet melting into one, like pure
> and heart-rending harmony. This is the Word of God. The whole
> creation is nothing but its vibration. When human music in its great-
> est purity pierces the soul, this is what we hear through it.[10]

Trying, as a man, to explore Wendy's exposition of the mystery
of the feminine, clearly addressed primarily to a group of women—
perhaps a group of Sisters of the Love of God at Fairacres—I find
myself strangely *included* in what Wendy has to say. It is partly because, though for women and about femininity, Wendy turns aside
from time to time to address aspects of the relationship between men
and women. But more deeply, I think it is that, in discussing the mystery of the feminine, Wendy is discussing what it is to be human, and
being human is being part of something that is marked by the poles
of masculine and feminine—whether one is a man or a woman. This
complementarity is of the essence of being human—being male in relation to the female, or female in relation to the male. So seeking to
understand the mystery of being feminine may well help me, a man,
to understand what it is to be masculine (though to speak of the 'mystery of the masculine' is not, perhaps, at all a natural way of putting
it), and also to help me understand what may be called elements of
the feminine within me.

There is a passage in the report on men and women in ministry
to which Wendy contributed, actually in the chapter on the Holy

---

[10] Simone Weil, *Waiting on God* (London: Routledge and Kegan Paul Ltd,
1951), '82–3' (actually p. 68), quoted in 'Sounding Stones', 61–2.

Trinity, which seeks to express the complementarity of men and women in their turning to God. It is too long to quote here, and though I cannot imagine that the passage does not owe something to Wendy, I can hear what seem to me discordant notes—not contradictory, but out of tune—that are a further reason for not quoting it.[11] What the implications of masculine/feminine complementarity are for the question of the ordination to the priesthood is not raised by Wendy. What is quite clear from what Wendy says, however, is the much more important issue of allowing the mystery of the feminine to inform the Church's understanding of itself. How far the Orthodox Church—that 'strange Orthodox Church, so poor and so weak'—is from even beginning at any official level to acknowledge what Wendy so eloquently sketched in 'Sounding Stones' was evident at the Great Synod of Crete (which Wendy did not live to see), at which women constituted a resounding absence.[12]

---

[11] It can be found on p. 30 of the report, Rowell, *Fearful Symmetry*.

[12] See, also, *The Reception of the Holy and Great Council: Reflections of Orthodox Christian Women*, ed. Carrie Frederick Frost (New York: Greek Orthodox Archdiocese of America: Department of Inter-Orthodox, Ecumenical and Interfaith Relations, 2018). This is a remarkable collection of reflections on the Council, in which the anger of behalf of Orthodox women at their exclusion from the Council, while perceptible, does not prevent a sense of hope and even confidence for the future.

11
SILENCE

The last essay of Wendy's that I want to discuss is 'Exploring Silence'.[1] We have already encountered the notion of silence several times in our exploration of Wendy's published work. It was clearly important to her, but it was more than that: Wendy seemed to inhabit silence. When talking to her, whether one-to-one or in a group discussion, her affinity with silence manifested itself in two ways. First, the attention she brought to the conversation or discussion she was engaged in seemed to grow from silence; she could listen; she did not seem, as so many people do, to be waiting for an opportunity to 'have her say'; sometimes, indeed, it seemed that she could wait and listen until whoever she was talking to had arrived where they needed to arrive—had, as it were, discovered what she or he needed to know. In this sense she was profoundly maieutic, an exemplar of the Socratic quality she so much prized. But secondly, her inhabiting silence seemed to manifest itself when she was moved to say something: her words seemed to come from a still point within herself, a place of calm, rather than from some still-unresolved argument. Perhaps it is only another way of putting it, that in her listening to another, she was able to hear, not just what was said, but a kind of margin that could not be expressed, but only, and rather dimly, felt. Sometimes she seemed to have that capacity for clairvoyance that enabled her to see and apprehend what the person concerned could not bring to expression: that quality of clairvoyance sometimes seen in the elders, for which, in recent times, St Porphyrios the Kavsokalyvite was well known.

---

[1] In *Cosmos, Crisis & Christ*, 63–92.

The pamphlet has an icon on the front cover, made by Wendy's godmother, Militza Zernov, called the 'Icon of 'Perfect' [or, more accurately, Blessed] Silence', variant of the 'Icon of Christ the Wisdom of God'. From the beginning, Wendy makes clear that her subject is, if not silence as prayer, an approach to silence that is never far from prayer. 'Prayer seems to be both an art, open to the deepest creative impulses in our being, and a discipline involving rhythm, accepting the systole and diastole, the ebb and flow.'[2] And she goes on to say, 'Of one thing I am sure: that I find it easier to talk *to* God than I do to talk *about* God, and I know that I am not alone in this'. (Indeed, she is not: she is in very good company indeed: in an early letter to Barlaam, the opponent of hesychasm, St Gregory Palamas warns him that 'it is dangerous to speak *about* God, if one does not know how to speak *to* God'). Nevertheless for many of us, she remarks, there seems to fall a shadow between what we experience in our religious or spiritual life and our everyday existence; which Stevie Smith captures in her poem:

I was much too far out all my life
And not waving but drowning.[3]

Such considerations introduce us to the way in which seeking an inner silence in prayer may provide a way of healing and uniting bits of me that seem a long way from each other. And perhaps it is the silence that makes this possible, for 'in some mysterious way, I think that what begins to happen is that not only do we begin to explore silence, but silence begins to explore us'.[4]

Wendy then goes on to explore different aspects of silence: allowing things to happen (rather than seeking to be always in control); being present where we are, in the course of which she quotes a couple of Hasidic tales which make the point that 'God meets us where we are,

---

[2] 'Exploring Silence', 66.
[3] 'Not Waving, but Drowning', in Stevie Smith, *Selected Poems*, ed. James MacGibbon (Penguin, 1978), 167, quoted in 'Exploring Silence', 67.
[4] 'Exploring Silence', 68.

and not where we are not, or when we are only half there';[5] entering into silence — different ways in which we can 'tune in' to silence, and escape 'my internal chatter' to find something deeper. In this context Wendy speaks of the way in which most of us have a propensity for one of the senses: touch, for instance, made use of in praying with a prayer rope or rosary; or the way in which one emotion or another becomes dominant so that one is drowned in it — 'an anxiety obsesses me; a depression darkens me; a joy unearths me … it is no good fighting', Wendy says, 'the more I scold myself, the more stubborn they become'[6] (recall what Wendy said in *Encountering Depression* about the necessity to accept our moods if we are to understand ourselves). Another section is called 'The Eternal Listener in Silence': as Wendy puts it, 'in the Christian tradition, silence is more often associated with the image of a listening companion than with a place emptied of sound'.[7] And then a section entitled 'Sifting Silence', or rather being sifted by the silence — as the old Quakers used to say. Such sifting is painful, and we need to 'hold on very hard in order to accept the depths of this search for the inner reality which silence explores in us', which will sometimes take us to places we have, as it were, 'padlocked up' so as to prevent our ever going there again. 'We don't want to know, and yet we must'. Sometimes we need someone else to hold on for us. Sometimes in this sifting we encounter betrayal, being betrayed, but also our betraying others: and there we need love and forgiveness, but not as acquisitions, but as gifts: 'Learning to face the betrayer and the betrayed in me can put me in touch with my need for these gifts, through my sorrow and suffering and my objective turning to God.'[8]

Silence has different 'shapes', as Wendy put it; she listed them as:

- 'The silence of availability', what Gabriel Marcel called *disponibilité*; the 'silence of growth', of gestation, of waiting and

---

[5] 'Exploring Silence', 70.

[6] Idem, 72.

[7] Idem, 74.

[8] Idem, 77.

endurance; 'silence beyond words', pure silence, the silence between lovers; and the 'silence of the Pietà' — of suffering and the mystery of death.

- 'Enduring silence' — carrying doubt, which turns out to be part of the 'journey into a living faith'; even in the final pericope of St Matthew's Gospel, when the risen Jesus manifests himself on a mountain in Galilee to his disciples, we read, When they saw him, they worshipped him; but some doubted' (Matt. 28:17).

- 'Living with silence' — 'Truly you are a God who hides himself' — *deus absconditus*, 'so silent as to frighten us into thinking that God has gone' — the archetypal form of the modern condition, drawn from Jean Paul's Christ's realization on the Cross that 'God is dead',[9] a realization on which Auschwitz seems to have set its seal:

> How is life with God still possible in a time in which there is an Auschwitz? ... The estrangement has become too cruel, the hiddenness too deep ... dare we urge the survivors, 'Call to him for he is kind; his mercy endures forever?'[10]

- 'Presence in silence' — 'to experience prayer as an unending pursuit of the Presence': 'The silence is the place of the Presence, and at its heart is God'.[11] This leads Wendy to speak of the Hebrew sense of the Name, the Name of God pronounced and effecting His Presence, and the use among Christians, especially the Orthodox, of the Jesus Prayer, the pronouncing of the Name of Jesus — a kind of 'speech-act', in which we evoke, or even better *enact* the presence of the one named, the Lord Jesus.

---

9 Jean Paul, *Siebenkäs [Blumen-, Frucht- und Dornenstücke oder Ehestand, Tod und Hochzeit des Armenadvokaten F. St. Siebenkäs im Reichsmarktflecken Kuhschnappel]* (Berlin, 1797), in the chapter 'The Dead Christ Proclaims That There Is No God'.

10 Martin Buber, *The Eclipse of God: Studies in the Relationship Between Religion and Philosophy* (New York: Harper, 1952), 132. Quoted in 'Exploring Silence', 82.

11 'Exploring Silence', 82.

There is a phrase, nexus mysteriorum, once much used, I believe, which is an attempt to express the internal consistency and inter-relatedness of the ultimate mysteries of the world. The Jesus Prayer is certainly one of the ways in which we can experience this nexus. The movement of the prayer is infinite because it increasingly puts in the heart of our being the silent heart of all being, the Divine Name.[12]

- 'Shared Silence': 'Although the journey into God is one that we must each undertake individually, in ever-increasing depth, yet we know that we are also called together; we need each other, we are inescapably part of each other.'[13] Wendy speaks of the prayer hours of a contemplative community, of the Communion of Saints, of Michael Polanyi's notion of the 'tacit dimension', of encounters in which silence achieves more than any words, of Quaker accounts of corporate silence. She ends by quoting a long passage from a section of Fr Gilbert Shaw's *The Face of Love*, adapted by Mother Mary Clare of the Sisters of the Love of God from his teaching, one stanza of which reads:

> Cleanse the complex patterns of my unconsciousness
>   that nothing may distort my will
>   or turn my heart from loving you,
>   from serving you in spirit and in truth.[14]

---

[12] 'Exploring Silence', 84.
[13] Idem, 86.
[14] Quoted in 'Exploring Silence', 90.

12
Beyond the 'Pamphlets'

Hitherto, I have relied mostly on the collection of Wendy's pamphlets that Hilary (her son) and Mother Katharine Hall confided to me shortly after her death. In addition, there are at least two pieces of her writing that were not published as pamphlets: she contributed an essay, 'Mary, the Flower and Fruit of Worship: The Mother of God in the Orthodox Tradition', to the *Festschrift* for Bishop (later Metropolitan) Kallistos Ware, *Abba: The Tradition of Orthodoxy in the West* (2003) and had a poem, 'Autolycus: Old Crow', published in *Agenda* 43 — an issue appropriately called 'Lauds'. The poem is reproduced below.

Wendy's *Festschrift* essay on the Mother of God includes much that we have already encountered, especially in *Windows for the Soul* and 'Sounding Stones', but one immediately notices a more formal structure than we have found in what were, for the most part, originally talks. Her essay begins by evoking in the context of Mariology a theme, characteristic of her whole approach to theology, that we can only approach the Mother of God 'with more silence than words', and that the only words we can find are 'held in cupped hands, out of the great sea of meanings which flows all around her'; for both East and West she is 'the star of that sea, the guide for lost and weary travellers'.[1] However, Wendy remarks, for many women in our age, her star 'has not been visible through the lowering clouds of controversy, anger and painful searching about the place of meaning of women and men together in the Church'. The trouble with Mary, from Wendy's perspective, is not directly so much to do with Mariology

---

[1] This and the following quotations in this paragraph are from 'Mary, the Flower and Fruit of Worship', in *Cosmos, Crisis & Christ*, 94.

(though that it has been deeply problematical for many can scarcely be ignored), but with the storm engendered by modernity and post-modernity. The impact of this storm, which has been felt in the Church, is closely bound up with matters of gender, the long-term inequality of the sexes, and the long, baleful shadow of patriarchal society. Very soon, Wendy takes the direction indicated by her title, and considers the presence of Mary in the liturgy: always there, always 'pointing beyond herself to Christ', and leading us 'to the place of the heart, the deep centre of our theandric personality … herself a living symbol of hesychia, or inner silence'. Wendy then goes on to remark that Mary 'does not belong to the outer world of declared dogma but to the secret inner life of the Church, to be discovered there. She is present as the flower and fruit of worship, ripened in tradition'. (Echoes of St Basil the Great and Vladimir Lossky will be evident to many of her readers.) The secret realm is manifest, first and foremost, in stories and song: the stories found, for example, in the *Protevangelium of James*, which have had such a profound influence in the liturgical celebration of Mary in the Churches of the East, and the songs of the Church, especially rich among the Orthodox. 'This deepest level of the human soul is where *poesis* happens — a creative energy which throws up for us dreams and images and is symbol-making and story-telling,' Wendy comments, and a little later she continues, 'That deep place of making gives rise to thought but it is wise for thought to keep its tap root in the creative matrix, where truths are invocatory, celebratory, proclamatory, rather than set out as rational propositions'. And so pre-eminently in the case of the Mother of God,

> There is a certain silence around her mysteries. Yet this numinous, awe-inspiring and luminous, light-giving silence has always been endlessly inspirational. One moment we have teaching on the apophatic need to move beyond images, to honour silence and venerate mysteries. The next moment we have images pouring forth as if from a breathtaking treasure-house.[2]

---

[2] 'Mary, the Flower and Fruit of Worship', 96.

There follow examples of the profusion of images that we find in celebration of the Mother of God in the Orthodox Liturgy: first, quoting from the Akathist Hymn, and then, exploring Mary's grief at the death of Christ, in the canon read as part of Compline on Good Friday. Here we find, Wendy suggests, 'a deep experience of feminine discourse that we otherwise meet in the rituals, rhythms and repetitions around the birth and nurture of small babies and children, as well as in expressions of grief and mourning around death'.[3] By these examples Wendy points to a 'matrix' in worship where we 'meet the Mother of God as the pivotal point through which we turn, bringing the cosmos with us, through our personhood, towards God, offering ourselves through her'—illustrated by one of the *stichera* sung at the Vesperal Liturgy of the Nativity of the Lord, in which, among the offerings of the whole of creation, we humans offer a 'Virgin Mother'. For her, Wendy tells us, the experience of all this in participating in the liturgical rites has been 'a transformative experience … as woman, as psychotherapist and as a human person, caught up in the theandric vision of what it means to be truly human', and she reflects briefly on the struggle she feels in herself as she experiences something that for many others (not least, women) seems alienating—something that many Orthodox are unwilling even to admit, save as an effect of 'secularized feminism'.

'Alone of all her sex', this phrase—the translation of a line from a poem by the ninth-century Irish poet, Caelius Sedulius (Scottus), famously used by Marina Warner as the title for her celebrated book on Mariology[4]—'encapsulates the danger, as women see it, that sometimes the Mother of God is celebrated as so special, so different, that we lose a sense of her solidarity with us and that is an appalling loss'.[5] Wendy reflects on the way Mary is presented—in poetry and art—as the fulfilment of a certain male idealization of what women

---

[3] This and the following quotations in this paragraph are from 'Mary, the Flower and Fruit of Worship', 97–8.

[4] Marina Warner, *Alone of all her Sex: The Myth and the Cult of the Virgin Mary* (London: Weidenfeld and Nicolson, 1976; 2nd edn: OUP, 2013).

[5] 'Mary, the Flower and Fruit of Worship', 99.

should be: 'quiet, preferably silent, humble, pure and good, in a domestic interior, devoted and submissive, knowing her place' (and also, one might add, biddable and pliant to male desire). And there is the fact, not often mentioned, that patristic and medieval images of Mary—in literature and art—are virtually all images created by men, *males*. Wendy tries to feel her way through this, focusing less on *what* the Virgin was, than on *who* she was (or is):

> We speak of her three-fold virginity—the one who was given to God, in innocence, in experience and ever. The 'everness' informs all the rest: a total givenness to God. Here we sense that virginity is not a state, and is certainly not a possession, but is rather an eschatological reality… a reality that calls to us from the fulness of time … from the way things will be because that is how they truly are ontologically.[6]

(Note that last word.) Wendy goes on to reflect on what is meant by this—for our understanding of the Mother of God, as well as for our understanding of what is means to make of our lives 'a theandric reality'—of this existential and eschatological sense of virginity as 'something into which we must grow': 'an ascetic path which can include all our brokenness, all the consequences of the Fall'. As Wendy pursues this, she enters into considerations we have already encountered in her meditations in *Windows for the Soul*: her reflections on annunciation—'the unprayable / Prayer at the calamitous annunciation'—'the undeniable / Clamour of the bell of the last annunciation' —'the hardly, barely prayable / Prayer of the one Annunciation', in T. S. Eliot's words in *Dry Salvages*, II: three annunciations.[7] Here she comments on a 'lifetime of annunciations' (her expression, though attributed to Eliot) saying that,

---

[6] 'Mary, the Flower and Fruit of Worship', 102.

[7] The quotation from *Four Quartets* that Wendy gives is a 'lifetime of annunciations', which, as I have noted above, I cannot find; there are, however, in section II of *The Dry Salvages*, as indicated above, three evocations of the annunciation: 'the calamitous', 'the last' and 'the One Annunciation'. Perhaps Wendy had these three 'annunciations' in mind and this is the source of the 'lifetime of annunciations'.

We meet each other and have to make something of what has come, however strange and alien it may seem at first—painful decision by painful decision sometimes. In the end, the annunciation we have to take on is death: how to give birth to the fact of one's own death? As Eliot said, 'The bone's prayer to Death is God. Only the hardly, barely prayable/Prayer of the one Annunciation'.[8]

There are other 'annunciations' that 'bring rejoicing'; Wendy presses on to consider the Mother of God, setting off to visit her cousin Elizabeth—visitation as annunciation, as it were—'saddl[ing] up her donkey and set[ting] out for the hill country'—a 'travelling woman, who can travel with searching women today',[9] to the Mother of God as 'one who could make something of the dark times ... who learnt to take the hard sayings and "treasure them in her heart"', able to 'endure not just our own suffering but the suffering of the Beloved': 'Mary found a way that kept her nailed to the foot of the Cross, when that was what was happening', leading Wendy back again in the Liturgy, to conclude that, 'The "feminine matrix" that her feasts give in liturgical form in the Orthodox tradition is a deeply satisfying resource for women in the Orthodox Church as it is for men.' Acknowledging that there 'may have to be transformations in the cultural application of some of the images', Wendy affirms that 'the Presence of the Mother of God transcends them all with her "Protecting Veil" that encompasses us all'.[10]

This is a remarkably rich essay on the Orthodox understanding of the Mother of God, which both places devotion to the Mother of God firmly in its Orthodox liturgical 'matrix', and leads the reader to face squarely real problems with the way in which images of the Virgin Mother have served (sometimes unconsciously) limited or dis-torted ends, in the end finding resolution by homing in on a kind of healing through suffering that lies at the heart of the mystery of the Mother of God.

---

[8] 'Mary, the Flower and Fruit of Worship', 104.

[9] Idem, 105.

[10] Idem, 107.

'AUTOLYCUS: OLD CROW'

Prelude

Autolycus, Old Crow:
Prompt—Fridays –
Platform 5, 7.25 –
Each time, for months,
I caught the 7.35—Because my sister was dying:

To the North

You flap in—ancient
Slightly crazed landing
Like an Old Lancaster.
You set about it –
Life –
Head thrusting back and forth,
Back and forth –
To persuade your body
To come along with you –
Me too:
The weight of Things –
A heavy rocking
Of grief not birth.

Not much on offer –
We both pecked
For crumbs of comfort –
Autolycus, Old Crow,
Carrion comfort,
Comfort in woe.

Weakly, weekly, I wanted to bring you –
Extras.
But it wouldn't do.
Death and scarcity have to be lived –
Some—how?

Postlude

Months later:
Not your time –
Not your platform,
I took the 10.45 to London –
You flapped in awkwardly –
Landing within an inch of my foot.
You may be a snapper-up
Of ill-considered trifles,
But you know how it is,
Between this world and the next –
Autolycus, Old Crow

    Autolycus, Old Crow,
    Crow come lately,
    Crow come soon –
    Never come never –
    Crow come.

This poem was published in the Spring 2008 issue of *Agenda*, a poetry magazine founded in 1959 by William Cookson at the instigation of Ezra Pound: it is a serious, modernist journal, not infrequently devoting an issue (or series of issues) to a particular poet, such as Ezra Pound, Geoffrey Hill (as early as 1979) and David Jones (who contributed visually to the journal, notably the representation of the title,

Agenda, on the cover page, and several times the whole cover design).[11] Wendy's poem must have been accepted with alacrity, as the datable event in the poem is the death of her sister Jillianne on 31 October 2006: 'To the North', the title of the main part of the poem, refers to her visits to the North of England, where her sister continued to live, to visit her while she was dying; these visits were evidently over, when the poem was written. I have no knowledge of any other poems by Wendy, but I have only been working from her published works; it would be very interesting to know if there are poems and drafts of poems in her notebooks and papers. It seems to me the work of a capable and practised poet, not a 'one-off'. One feature of the poem also found in her letters (and to an extent in her talks and papers) is her 'signature punctuation mark': the dash! Thinking back on some of the longer letters I had from Wendy, it seems to me that there is a fine line between her published poem, 'Autolycus: Old Crow', and the way she expressed herself in her letters: moving from image to image, with a development that is almost that of a story-teller, from evocation to evocation, linked by association of ideas—the movement of something more like a story than an argument—a sequence of images and observations (in the sense of attention to particular things seen) loosely held together in something resembling a narrative. As to influences, Ted Hughes comes to my mind, but that is because I know how much Wendy was attracted to his verse and, I suppose, the word 'crow'. This solitary poem begs to be found among further examples of Wendy's poetry which might, one day, come to light.

---

[11] For information about the genesis of *Agenda*, see William Cookson's account in *Agenda: An Anthology. The First Four Decades 1959–1993*, ed. William Cookson (Manchester: Carcanet, 1994), xiii–xxvi.

13
CONCLUSION

I am not sure what I have achieved in this essay; possibly no more than transferring Wendy's reflections from the form they naturally took, uniquely Wendy's, to something more academic, not in the least uniquely mine. There seems to me no point in summarizing what I have attempted to say: Wendy's 'infinite variety' prevents that. I had thought to say something about the people that inhabited her thought-world either through conversation or reading, but they have mostly appeared in their own right, and I am sure those mentioned are only the tip of the iceberg, for she knew many people, and read widely—from childhood when she discovered she had the 'bookshop gene', which she noticed in her children and grandchildren. I began by recalling her self-designation as a 'walking ecumenical movement', and how she never lost any of the forms of religious life that she had experienced. In some of the later pieces (actually I think they may be part of the same occasion, but it is not clear) Wendy began to speak of aging, growing old—she would have been coming up to 73 at the time of one discussion, which I suspect followed an occasion when she gave a talk that was published as 'A Journey to the Russian Orthodox Church':

> It was that phrase,
> > *at the turn of the tide you will be by my side*
> > > and you know that feeling at my age, as with many of you here, about the tide turning.[1]

---

[1] Discussion in the Conference Room at Ditchingham, Sunday 3 June 2007 (I think this was the discussion that accompanied the 'Journey', the other place where she talks about getting older: see 'Journey', 15).

She goes on to speak of how, when young, we are concerned with who we are, but that we reach a turning point later on when we are concerned about what it means to be human, what it means to be alive, what it means to be a man or a woman. She said this, I feel, not in a spirit of resignation, but, as it were, looking forward to this next approaching stage of her rich life. She had only another six years or so of her earthly journey left, and it is now ten years since her death — time enough for an attempt to be made to record something of what she meant to those who were privileged to know her.

PUBLICATIONS BY WENDY ROBINSON

'Alcoholism: Community and After-care Aspects', *Journal of Addiction*, 59:2 (1963), 81–91.

'Autolycus: Old Crow', *Agenda*, vol. 43, nos. 2–3 (Spring 2008), 96–7.

'Basic Psycho-Social Characteristics of the Battered Child Syndrome', co-author Joan Court, *Update* (1971) [GP's Journal].

'The Battered Child Syndrome', co-author Joan Court, *Midwives Chronicle and Nursing Notes*, 95 (July 1970), 196.

The Chaplain and the Social Worker, *Free Church Quarterly* (1973).

Cosmos, Crisis & Christ: Essays of Wendy Robinson, collected and edited by Andrew Louth, Fairacres Publications 211 (Oxford: SLG Press, 2024).

Dreamwork and Prayer, co-author David Holt, Guild of Pastoral Psychology Lecture, no. 194 (London: Guild of Pastoral Psychology, 1978).

Exploring Silence, Fairacres Publications 170 (Oxford: SLG Press, 2013), new edition in *Cosmos, Crisis & Christ*, 63–92.

Bishop Geoffrey Rowell, ed., *A Fearful Symmetry? The Complementarity of Men and Women in Ministry*, contributors: A. M. Allchin, Sandra Figges, Bishop Kallistos of Diokleia, Wendy Robinson, Geoffrey Rowell, Stephen Verney, Rosemary Wickremansinghe, Linda Woodhead, Graham Woolfenden (London: SPCK, 1992).

'The Ground of our Being: A Study of Hidden Consciousness', *Unpublished paper read at the Conference of the Association of Orthodox Christian Psychotherapists* (2009).

A Journey to the Russian Orthodox Church: An Ecumenical Journey into Orthodoxy (London: Servants of Christ the King Pamphlets, 2007), new edition in *Cosmos, Crisis & Christ*, 1–16.

The Lost Traveller's Dream: Developing a Theology for Working with Mental Illness, Occasional Papers in Christian Counselling, no. 1 (Oxford: Oxford Christian Institute for Counselling, 1995), new edition in *Cosmos, Crisis & Christ*, 33–48.

'Mary, the Flower and Fruit of Worship: The Mother of God in the Orthodox Tradition', in *Abba: The Tradition of Orthodoxy in the West. Festschrift for Bishop Kallistos Ware*, ed. John Behr, Andrew Louth, Dimitri Conomos (Crestwood, NY: SVSP, 2003), 193–205, new edition in *Cosmos, Crisis & Christ*, 93–108.

'From Metaphor to Symbol in Creative Writing', *2011 conference of the Association of Orthodox Christian Psychotherapists on 'Symbols and Symbolism': Conference Proceedings* (privately published *c.* 2012).

Gonville ffrench-Beytagh, *Out of the Depths: Encountering Depression*, Fairacres Publications 162 (Oxford: SLG Press, 1990), epilogue.

Pastoral Counselling: An Exercise in Ontology, co-author David Holt (Oxford: ZiPrint, 1980).

'The Quest for the Heart of the Work: An Ontological Approach to Spirituality and Psychotherapy/Counselling', *Psychodynamic Counselling* 4/3 (August 1998), 335–48, new edition in *Cosmos, Crisis & Christ*, 17–32.

'Reflections: sub specie aeternitatis', *Contact*, 126:1 (1998), 30–1.

Search for Meaning, co-author Christopher R. Bryant, Guild of Pastoral Psychology Lecture, no. 196 (London: The Guild of Pastoral Psychology, 1979).

Sounding Stones: Reflections on the Mystery of the Feminine, Fairacres Publications 99 (Oxford: SLG Press, 1987), new edition in *Cosmos, Crisis & Christ*, 49–62.

Windows for the Soul. Living with Icons (London: Servants of Christ the King, 2007, printed 2020).

SLG PRESS PUBLICATIONS

www.slgpress.co.uk

CONTEMPLATIVE POETRY SERIES

CP1	*Amado Nervo: Poems of Faith and Doubt*	trans. John Gallas (2021)
CP2	*Anglo-Saxon Poets: The High Roof of Heaven*	trans. John Gallas (2021)
CP3	*Middle English Poets: Where Grace Grows Ever Green*	ed. John Gallas (2021)
CP4	*Selected Poems: The Voice inside Our Home*	Edward Clarke (2022)
CP5	*Women & God: Drops in the Sea of Time*	trans. and ed. John Gallas (2022)
CP6	*Gabrielle de Coignard & Vittoria Colonna: Fly Not Too High*	trans. John Gallas (2022)
CP7	*Selected Poems: Chancing on Sanctity*	James Ramsay (2022)
CP8	*Gabriela Mistral: This Far Place*	trans. John Gallas (2023)
CP9	*Henry Vaughan & George Herbert: Divine Themes and Celestial Praise*	ed. Edward Clarke (2023)
CP10	*Love Will Come with Fire*	SISTERS OF THE LOVE OF GOD (2023)
CP11	*Touchpapers*	collected and trans. John Gallas (2023)
CP12	*Seasons of my Soul*	Clare McKerron (2023)
CP13	*Reinhard Sorge: Take Flight to God*	trans. John Gallas (2024)
CP14	*Embertide: Encountering Saint Frideswide*	Romola Parish (2024)
CP15	*Thomas Campion: Made All of Light*	ed. Julia Craig-McFeely (2024)

VESTRY GUIDES

VG1	*The Visiting Minister: How to Welcome Visiting Clergy to Your Church*	Paul Monk (2021)
VG2	*Help! No Minister! or Please Take the Service*	Paul Monk (2022)
VG3	*The Liturgy of the Eucharist: An Introductory Guide*	Paul Monk (2024)

www.slgpress.co.uk